The Complete Guide to

Growing and Using Sprouts

Everything You Need to
Know Explained Simply —

Including Easy-to-Make Recipes

By Richard Helweg

THE COMPLETE GUIDE TO GROWING AND USING SPROUTS: EVERY-
THING YOU NEED TO KNOW EXPLAINED SIMPLY —
INCLUDING EASY-TO-MAKE RECIPES

Copyright © 2011 Atlantic Publishing Group, Inc.
1405 SW 6th Avenue • Ocala, Florida 34471 • Phone 800-814-1132 • Fax 352-622-1875
Web site: www.atlantic-pub.com • E-mail: sales@atlantic-pub.com
SAN Number: 268-1250

Library of Congress Cataloging-in-Publication Data

Helweg, Richard, 1956-
 The complete guide to growing and using sprouts : everything you
need to know explained simply : including easy to make recipes / by
Richard Helweg.
     p. cm.
 Includes bibliographical references and index.
 ISBN-13: 978-1-60138-340-2 (alk. paper)
 ISBN-10: 1-60138-340-1 (alk. paper)
 1. Sprouts--Varieties. 2. Sprouts--Nutrition. 3. Cookery (Sprouts)
I. Title.
 SB324.53.H45 2010
 635--dc22
                                2010017436

PROJECT MANAGER: Amy Moczynski • amoczynski@atlantic-pub.com
PEER REVIEWER: Marilee Griffin • INTERIOR DESIGN: Rhana Gittens

Printed on Recycled Paper

Printed in the United States

We recently lost our beloved pet "Bear," who was not only our best and dearest friend but also the "Vice President of Sunshine" here at Atlantic Publishing. He did not receive a salary but worked tirelessly 24 hours a day to please his parents. Bear was a rescue dog that turned around and showered myself, my wife, Sherri, his grand-parents Jean, Bob, and Nancy, and every person and animal he met (maybe not rabbits) with friendship and love. He made a lot of people smile every day.

We wanted you to know that a portion of the profits of this book will be donated to The Humane Society of the United States. *–Douglas & Sherri Brown*

The human-animal bond is as old as human history. We cherish our animal companions for their unconditional affection and acceptance. We feel a thrill when we glimpse wild creatures in their natural habitat or in our own backyard.

Unfortunately, the human-animal bond has at times been weakened. Humans have exploited some animal species to the point of extinction.

The Humane Society of the United States makes a difference in the lives of animals here at home and worldwide. The HSUS is dedicated to creating a world where our relationship with animals is guided by compassion. We seek a truly humane society in which animals are respected for their intrinsic value, and where the human-animal bond is strong.

Want to help animals? We have plenty of suggestions. Adopt a pet from a local shelter, join The Humane Society and be a part of our work to help companion animals and wildlife. You will be funding our educational, legislative, investigative and outreach projects in the U.S. and across the globe.

Or perhaps you'd like to make a memorial donation in honor of a pet, friend or relative? You can through our Kindred Spirits program. And if you'd like to contribute in a more structured way, our Planned Giving Office has suggestions about estate planning, annuities, and even gifts of stock that avoid capital gains taxes.

Maybe you have land that you would like to preserve as a lasting habitat for wildlife. Our Wildlife Land Trust can help you. Perhaps the land you want to share is a backyard— that's enough. Our Urban Wildlife Sanctuary Program will show you how to create a habitat for your wild neighbors.

So you see, it's easy to help animals. And The HSUS is here to help.

2100 L Street NW • Washington, DC 20037 • 202-452-1100
www.hsus.org

Dedication

For my sprouts Aedan and Rory. Eat your greens!

Table of Contents

CHAPTER 8: Soups, Stews, and Chili   135

CHAPTER 12: Breads, Baked Goods, and Cereal   227

CHAPTER 13: Beverages   249

Foreword

Never before in our modern history has diet and health been such an important topic. As we learn more about how we truly are what we eat, many people are turning to fresh, organic, and raw foods. Although many people are learning how to grow food in small gardens, the time and energy devoted to growing your own food often proves to be too much work. Sprouting provides the solution.

It is important to have access to information that provides clear guidance when you branch out in a new direction or learn an unfamiliar skill. Without it, one can easily get discouraged or succumb to a feeling that trying something new is just too complicated or involves too much planning.

The Complete Guide to Growing and Using Sprouts can help you avoid all these pitfalls. Not only does this book show you a clear and concise overview of all the most common sprouting methods, but you will also learn delicious and fun ways to enjoy your sprouts, as well as what to do with your sprouts when they are ready.

When my company, SeThInk Media, agreed to produce and publish an informational DVD that featured a revolutionary "no rinse" sprouting method, our team's first task was to thoroughly research sprouts and sprouting methods. In this information age, information overload is a condition that all of us are faced with at one time or another, and our attempt to research sprouting and sprouting methods online proved to be a daunting task. Contradicting information, not knowing what is accurate, and the overwhelming number of websites that appeared in a search query were all frustrations that we encountered.

If we had found *The Complete Guide to Growing and Using Sprouts* back then, it would have saved us months of sifting through information on the Internet. While many publications are available on the basic techniques of sprouting, this book actually shows you the value of adding sprouts to your diet through the recipes and nutrition facts. Author Richard Helweg generously provides historical, scientific, and technical information to help ensure your success in becoming a happy sprouter.

Personally, I have prepared many of the recipes in this book, and I am consistently impressed with the tastes and textures that sprouts can add to any meal. My work with living foods has taught me that healthy food does not have to taste like "health food," and this book has helped me to take more pleasant steps down the path of health.

Happy Sprouting!

Daniel Cavallaro
President, SeThInk Media
Producer of Seeds of Sustainability Education Series Volume I:
The Marche Sprouting Method & Living Oils
www.seedsofsustainability.org

Introduction

If you are charged with shopping for your family's weekly groceries and you try to do your best to buy the freshest fruits and vegetables available, you know that this can be a bit of a challenge, especially in the winter months. If the head of lettuce you are considering traveled from somewhere far away to get to your store, you may have reservations about its freshness or its purity. The average distance produce travels from farm to grocer is 1,500 miles. When a head of lettuce travels 1,500 miles, how fresh can it be?

Now, think about the bountiful months of summer. You may have a healthy backyard garden. Perhaps you are near a local farmer's market where you can get to know the individuals that grow the produce you put on your table. Maybe you are a member of a Community Supported Agriculture (CSA) farm where you get regular deliveries of fresh produce. These are all very good ways to provide you and your family with the freshest of produce.

Even with the spread of farmer's markets and the growing popularity of backyard and community gardens, many of us just do not have the access to the fresh foods that we want. You may not have yards that can accommodate a garden. Where do you get fresh grown foods during the winter months?

The answer to this question rests in your hands: sprouts. You cannot get any fresher food than the sprouts that you grow in your kitchen, living room, or anywhere in your home. Even if you do not fancy yourself a gardener, you will be able to grow fresh sprouts and enjoy all the benefits that come with eating and cooking with these highly nutritious powerhouses of vitamins, minerals, antioxidants, proteins, and enzymes.

Humans have been growing and eating sprouted seeds for thousands of years. Bean sprouts have been a staple of Chinese cuisine for more than 5,000 years. The Chinese have used bean sprouts, specifically mung bean and soy bean, in their diet to calm digestive problems, bloating, rheumatoid arthritis, and nervousness. The Essenes, a Jewish religious sect that flourished around what is now Syria more than 2,000 years ago, made their daily bread using only sprouts. *Several recipes for Essene bread are included in the recipe section of this book.* More recently, sprouts were regularly used to provide essential vitamins to those on long sea voyages before the benefits of citrus were realized. It is known that Captain James Cook developed a vitamin supplement made of sprouted beans that he had his sailors consume during long sea voyages in the 18th century. This supplement provided a much needed source of vitamin C. Over the past 3,000 years, humans have used sprouts as an important source of vitamins, minerals, and protein because they are easy to produce and inexpensive.

Besides being nutritious, sprouts are inexpensive, easy to grow, and an incredibly versatile ingredient in a wide variety of healthy and tasty dishes. This book will take you step-by-step through the process of knowing what to sprout, how to sprout, and how to use the seeds, grains, legumes, and nuts you sprout. You will learn a variety of sprouting methods and ways to go beyond sprouts and develop shoots and small indoor greenhouse gardens. You will also find a wealth of tested and easy-to-follow recipes that will allow you to use your fresh sprouts.

The goal of this book is to give you everything you need to know to get started growing this most healthy of foods. This resource will also offer you case studies of individuals who have been growing and cooking with sprouts for many years. These case studies will offer advice on what to sprout and when to sprout it; how and why sprouts will make a difference in your diet; as well as some great recipes for using those sprouts.

One more suggestion for using this book: If you have kids, get them involved in sprouting. Besides the health benefits sprouts can offer everyone, there is a wonderful learning opportunity in growing sprouts. Sprouts are living things. Working with children in a garden is a great opportunity to experience the wonder of the cycle of life. It is also just great family fun that you can eat.

Chapter 1

The Story of a Sprout

> *"To see things in the seed, that is genius."*
> — Lao Tzu, Chinese philosopher

A seed is a beginning, as well as an ending. It is part of an ongoing life cycle: The seed grows into the plant that produces the seed and on and on. What great power that little seed must have. We all know the proverb, "From little acorns, mighty oaks do grow." This sentiment is just as true of sunflower seeds, wheat berries, and lentils, all of which hold the power of transformation.

The first step each of these seeds, grains, legumes, and nuts take in this life cycle of transformation is becoming a sprout. To **sprout** is to begin to grow from a seed, grain, legume, or nut. As this book proceeds, those will be our categories of designation.

Starting With Seeds

The sprout is the first stage of life after the seed. Seeds are dormant packets of energy; that is, they are asleep. Seeds can remain dormant for very long periods of time. In fact, scientists are still trying to answer the question relating to just how long seeds can remain dormant. Scientists have sprouted seeds that they know are 140 years old. Jane Shen-Miller, a research biologist at the University of California Los Angeles (UCLA), has a living seed from a dry lakebed in China that has been dated using carbon testing as more than 1,200 years old. A living seed is a seed that, while still dormant, is capable of sprouting.

All this points to a life force within a seed that is powerful and resilient. A sprout is what occurs the moment that dormant life force has been awakened. Sprouts of seeds, grains, legumes, and nuts require the life-giving power of water for this awakening. Hungarian biochemist Albert Szent-Györgyi, who won the 1937 Nobel Prize for Medicine, is quoted as saying, "Water is life's matter and matrix, mother and medium. There is no life without water." That is as true for humans as it is for seeds, grains, legume, and nuts.

To sprout a seed, you just need to add water. To test this, do a little experiment. Take one seed — any kind of seed will do — and drop it in a glass of water. Place the glass in a dark place, and after a few days (depending on the kind of seed you choose), a sprout will appear. Some seeds, grains, legumes, or nuts transform overnight. Red lentils will show sprouts in as little as 12 hours.

How a seed transforms into a sprout is a very complex tale that begins before the seed itself is produced. As the seed is a part of a cycle of life, saying that the seed comes before the plant is akin to saying that the egg came before the chicken. The seed was born by a plant that put all of its life's energies into making seeds. Making seeds ensures the plant will continue to thrive from generation to generation. In making the seed, the plant stored all the vitamins, minerals, proteins, fats, and carbohydrates necessary to give birth to another of its species. The plant packs the seed and casts it off to wait for just the right time and environment suitable for germination. To **germinate** is to sprout, and to sprout is to begin the life cycle anew.

As a sprouter, your task is to provide the environment suitable for germination. By providing that seed with "life's matter and matrix," which is water and air at a proper temperature, you allow that seed to begin to transform that stored energy into a growing life force.

Transforming From Seed to Sprout

How to set the life cycle in motion for seeds, grains, legumes, and nuts varies from seed to seed. Seeds, grains, legumes, and nuts all vary in their means of germination, depending on how the plant developed over its long history as a living organism. Some seeds have thin outer coats and will germinate very quickly with a little water and a relatively warm temperature. However, some seeds that require a longer germination time were developed to be ingested by animals, carried away from the plant that produced it, and dispersed far away after a long winter. Some seeds have developed a deep dormancy that protects the seed from sprouting in the late fall or winter, which would certainly not be beneficial to its continued survival. Some nuts, such as almonds, have very thin seed coats and require a very short germination time (one to two days). At the other end of the spectrum is the coconut, with a very thick coat, which takes about four months to sprout. Sprouted coconuts are considered a delicacy and taste delicious. *The ways of sprouting all of these different seeds, grains, legumes, and nuts will be described in Chapter 5.*

As the seed is sprouted, some very significant chemical changes begin to take place. The seed, with the help of water and air, begins to produce enzymes that are vital in converting the stored and concentrated nutrients into everything the seed will need to carry on the life cycle. **Enzymes** are proteins produced in living cells that speed up or increase the rate of a chemical reaction such as the metabolic processes of an organism. Enzymes can increase the speed of a chemical reaction by up to a million times more than normal. By introducing that little seed to water, you have set a miraculous force into motion.

There are many changes that the enzymes cause as a seed sprouts: The stored carbohydrates are being transformed into simple sugars; complex proteins are being turned into amino acids; fatty acids, vitamins, and minerals are all increasing at incredible rates; and the sprout takes minerals and other elements from the water and binds them to amino acids. All of these very complex activities are done to continue the plant's life cycle. These actions are also what make the sprout so beneficial to the human diet.

Sprouts are what are called a **biogenic food**, which means they are a living food. The primary reason that sprouts are such a healthy food is that they are capable of transferring the living energy that is within them to those who consume them. Ounce for ounce, there are more nutrients in sprouts than any other food source. Like energy in all food, the energy from sprouts is measured as calories. Sprouts have calories that are full of vitamins, minerals, protein, and many other good things. Calories can also be empty and lacking nutrients, such as those you get from drinking soda. However, the calories that come from eating sprouts are full of life.

Benefits of Sprouts

Humans have been eating sprouted seeds, grains, legumes, and nuts for thousands of years. There are records indicating that the Chinese have been growing and consuming bean sprouts for more than 5,000 years. Bean sprouts, as used by the Chinese, have long been considered to have great health benefits and have been used to guard against and cure many ailments. Sprouts have been used to reduce inflammation, cure rheumatism, and produce a laxative effect.

Recent studies have shown sprouts to have nearly miraculous health benefits. Researchers at Johns Hopkins University School of Medicine have shown that broccoli sprouts have an extremely high amount of a substance called sulforaphane. **Sulforaphane** is a natural cancer-fighting compound (a **compound** is a substance made up of two or more chemical elements) that has potent antioxidant effects and helps support detoxification. Scientists have known that broccoli contained high amount of sulforaphane, but recent testing has shown that broccoli sprouts and shoots contain 20 to 50 times more of the compound than mature broccoli. *You will read more about the benefits of specific sprouts in Chapter 3. Also, you will read more about the difference between sprouts and shoots in Chapter 4.*

In another study of broccoli sprouts, a researcher at the University of Saskatchewan has recently indicated that they may cut the risk of stroke, high blood pressure, and cardiovascular disease. The study suggests that broccoli sprouts raise the anti-inflammatory capacity of cells, thus providing the stated health benefits.

Other studies outlining the health benefits of sprouts are growing in number every day. Alfalfa sprouts, soybean sprouts, clover sprouts, and the sprouts of oil seeds such as flax contain phytoestrogens. **Phytoestrogens** are a group of compounds that plants produce and have similar characteristics to the human hormone estrogen. These phytoestrogens, namely isoflavones, coumestans, and lignans, have been shown to help guard against osteoporosis, cancer, and heart disease.

Besides the disease-fighting capacity of many types of sprouts, eating sprouts also has great dietary advantages. Lentil, mung bean, and soy bean sprouts are all very high in protein. Radish, mung bean, and soy bean sprouts all have significant supplies of vitamin C. Radish and onion sprouts have high supplies of vitamin A, and the list of other benefits sprouts can offer go on and on. What makes all of these advantages even more compelling is that sprouts, while extremely high in vitamins, minerals, protein, and dietary fiber, are low in calories and have no cholesterol. Sprouts are an important weapon in our national struggle against the epidemic of obesity and also helpful in preventing an increase in diabetes cases as obesity is a major cause of diabetes.

These are just the health benefits sprouts provide individuals. Some of these benefits, such as those used in the struggle against obesity and diabetes, also extend to communities. The cost of obesity and diabetes to communities and countries is staggering and continues to grow.

Another way that growing sprouts affects communities is that sprouting is an extremely environmentally friendly practice as it requires no land, no fossil fuel, produces no waste, utilizes no chemicals, and provides an extremely high level of food fuel energy. No other food you prepare, buy, and/or consume can make as positive a claim as sprouts do.

Another positive addition to this growing list of reasons to grow sprouts is that they are good for your pets. There is also a long list of sprouted seeds, grains, legumes and nuts veterinarians recommend for dogs and cats. The health benefits sprouts offer our pets mirror those for humans. Alfalfa, barley, flax, garlic, millet, quinoa, and wheat are all sprouts and shoots that vets will recommend as part of a healthy diet for dogs, cats, and birds.

When you consider all of the benefits of sprouting described above, perhaps the one benefit that ties the whole benefits package together is the economic advantages sprouting offers. This book will explore the costs associated with sprouting systems in Chapter 2, but the cost of seeds versus the benefits they provide appears to be what one might call "a no-brainer." For example, a pound of organic wheat berries costs $1.29, but after sprouting, wheat berries may multiply in weight by ten times. In this case, a pound of sprouted wheat costs about 13 cents a pound and is a good source of protein, carbohydrates, is low in cholesterol, high in iron, and a great source of trace minerals. Another example might be that a pound of organic raw sunflower seeds costs $3.29 a pound, but after sprouting, the seeds multiply their weight by nine times. The resulting cost of a pound of sprouted sunflower seeds is 36 cents a pound for a food that is an extremely high source of protein (three times higher than wheat) with exceptionally high mineral levels, and high levels of vitamins A, E, D, and the complete range of B vitamins. Beyond this, sprouted sunflower seeds are rich in chlorophyll that has a positive effect on the liver and blood. Another benefit these seeds possess? Sprouted sunflower seeds are delicious.

The genius in the seed is that it is alive, nutritious, has great health benefits for humans and animals, is environmentally friendly, and is economically practical. Also, they taste great.

Before you learn how to grow the little powerhouses that are sprouts, it is important that you know what exactly is going on inside that seed that makes it sprout. To understand the anatomy of the seed is to understand its capability.

Anatomy of a Seed

The true blessing of the seed is the miracle of what the seed holds. It was stated previously that plants live to create those seeds, grains, legumes, and nuts that will ensure their survival as a species. While it is true that not all plants produce seeds to reproduce, this section will examine plants that produce seeds; how those seeds are produced; how the seeds are dispersed; and how the seeds germinate to begin the life cycle anew.

In examining the entirety of the plant kingdom that produces seeds, you can separate those plants into two categories: plants that produce flowers and those that do not produce flowers. There is a category of plant that does not produce flowers or seeds (ferns, for example) and these plants reproduce via spores. There are a wide variety of plants that produce flowers, including apple trees, cacti, and pumpkins. Seed-bearing plants that do not produce flowers include coniferous trees like spruce trees and pine trees.

Pollination

Both flowering and non-flowering seed-producing plants follow a similar growth process, and both kinds of plants have male and female parts. Plants produce pollen (the male part) and a way to collect the pollen, such as a flower or, in the case of coniferous trees, cones (the female part). The wind, insects, or animals transfer pollen from plant to plant to fertilize the female part of the plant. After fertilization, seeds are produced.

Coniferous trees rely solely on the wind for pollination. The pollen is very light and light breezes can easily transport it. The cones of trees are sticky and easily catch the pollen that blows in the wind.

Flowering plants may be pollinated by pollen in the wind, but they also rely on bees, other insects, and animals as well. As bees gather nectar from flowers, they also gather pollen on their bodies and this pollen travels with them from plant to plant. Pollen fertilizes the plant, and after the plant is fertilized it creates seeds. Fertilized flowering plants create seeds in fruit and coniferous plants create the seed in their cones. The fruit and the cone are used to protect the seed. Contained within that seed is all the genetic information and plant energy required to make a new plant. When the seed matures to the point that it has collected all the information and energy that is required to grow a new plant, the mother plant casts the seed off to do its job of sprouting, growing, and keeping the cycle of life moving forward.

Because most plants are stationary and cannot travel from place to place, they count on animals and the wind to scatter their seeds. Sometimes the seed falls close to the mother plant, but sometimes a bird may eat the fruit containing the seed and fly a great distance to drop the seed many miles away. Or sometimes the seed is harvested for you to use in your kitchen and sprouting jar.

Seeds for sprouting come from flowering plants and coniferous plants. Some seeds sprout better than others and all seeds are not germinated in the same way, but all seeds are of a similar design and each viable seed has the ability to grow on to become a new plant, given the right conditions.

Germination

The best kind of seed to examine as you explore how a seed germinates is a bean. Beans are large compared to other seeds and it is relatively easy to open them and see what is going on inside. Also, beans have relatively thin coats, making them easy to open.

To see just how a bean germinates, fold and roll a thick paper towel so it conforms to the inside of a clear glass. Put some sand in the middle of the paper towel in the glass to hold the paper towel in its cylindrical shape as you will be wetting the towel. Place a bean (kidney or lima beans work well for this experiment) between the paper towel and the glass so you can see the bean. Moisten the paper towel with water. Place the glass in a dark cabinet and observe it over several days. You will see the bean sprout develop a root and begin to develop leaves.

To make this experiment a little more illustrative as to what is happening in that bean, take a second bean and slice it open to look inside. See what it looks like inside before it germinates. To make it easier to open, soak the bean overnight, which will cause it to soften and swell a little. Make a cut around the outer edge of the bean, avoiding the blemish where the bean was connected by the seed stalk to the inside of the pod. If you are using a larger bean like a lima bean, you should be able to identify this blemish. After you make the cut, you can easily remove the seed coat, which is called the **testa**. As you remove the testa, you will see a young root (called a **radicle**) that fits into the area where that small blemish is you did not cut. This is where the seed was attached to the pod. You might liken this to an umbilical cord because this is how the seed received nutrients from the mother plant.

You will find that you can split the inside of the bean into two halves, which are called the **cotyledons**. The cotyledons are the seed leaves and contain the stored energy the seed will need to grow into a plant. In other words, the cotyledon is the plant's food. Between the cotyledons is the tiny plant that will develop into a new bean plant. This is the tiny plant that you will see emerge from the bean in your glass experiment. This tiny plant is made up of a root and a **plumule** (shoot) that has small leaves.

When you grow and consume sprouts, you are consuming not only the young plant, but also the store of energy that is in the cotyledon. This is why sprouts have so much more nutritional value than mature plants.

After the mother plant has cast off the seed, its germination depends on the temperature and moisture of the environment in which it eventually lands. Warmer temperatures are generally more conducive to germination and seed growth. The germination process consists of the seed taking on water, which triggers the production of enzymes that convert the stored and concentrated nutrients into all the things the seed will need to carry on the life cycle. *This process was described earlier in this chapter.*

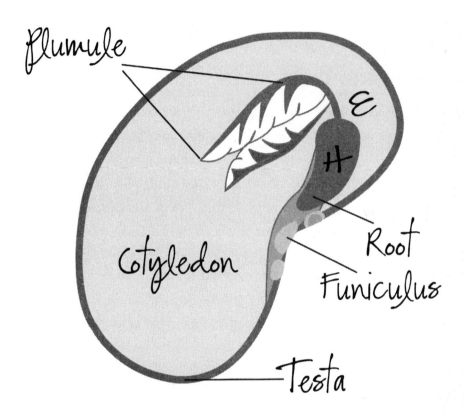

Sprouts versus shoots

As the seed feeds itself and that feeding increases, a root pushes through the testa. The root is the part of the plant that, if set in soil, travels down into the earth to anchor the plant and collect nutrients from the soil. This is a sprout. The water causes new growth to occur in the seed, which forms the sprout.

The part of the seed that will travel upward to collect nutrients from the sun and the air is the **plumule**. The plumule, if allowed to develop, will become a **shoot.** Thus, the new growth that will become the root is the sprout and the aerial part of the plant that will become a leaf is the shoot. This answers the question of what the difference is between sprouts and shoots.

Consuming Sprouts

When you grow and consume sprouts, you are consuming living plants. When you introduce these living things into your body, you are transferring their living energy into you. The vitamins, proteins, minerals, and living enzymes that are vital to the life of the young plant are active and at the peak of their nutritional value. Eating sprouts and shoots transfers the vitality and energy housed in the sprouts directly into your system.

Because you are consuming these young sprouts, it is said that you are **eating low** on the food chain. Simply explained, there is nothing standing between you and this basic source of energy. If, for example, you were to eat a steak from a cow that was grass-fed, the cow would be eating low on the food chain and you would be taking the energy the cow transformed from the grasses. In other words, you are eating higher up on the food chain than if you were only eating sprouts and vegetables. There is an argument that the lower you eat on the food chain, the healthier your diet is as you get the fundamental nutrients on a primary level as opposed to getting them secondarily. When you consume sprouts and eat low on the food chain, you are taking in far more nutrition and energy than is being spent to produce the food you eat.

Sometimes, it may not matter where you are eating on the food chain; what matters is the taste. You would probably not venture into this practice of growing your own sprouts if a sprout tasted absolutely awful. Because tastes differ from person to person, it is impossible to guarantee that you will love the taste of broccoli sprouts if you do not like the taste of broccoli. Broccoli sprouts, like broccoli, are more a matter of texture than taste. They do not taste exactly like broccoli, but have a clean and crisp texture as a food. As far as taste goes, sprouts will offer you either a more intense taste than their mature plants (as in radish sprouts), or a milder and subtler flavor (as in sprouted wheat). Again, everyone's tastes are different, so you are encouraged to experiment.

Now that you know the anatomy of the seed and what happens to make it sprout, it is time to know what you will need to get this action started. You will be surprised how simple it is to get this complex process underway.

Chapter 2

Sprouting Equipment

All you really need to get started growing your own sprouts is a jar, some seeds, and water. You can easily grow large amounts of sprouts for many years with only those three items. There are, however, a number of other items that you can employ to maintain an ongoing sprout- and shoot-growing operation. This chapter will define and describe just about everything that you could possibly use to grow all the sprouts you are ready to use.

Jars

There is not a specially designed jar for sprouting; any glass jar will do. That being said, there are a few things you should consider when you look for a jar that you may use for sprouting. Perhaps the most important thing about the jars you choose will be the size of the jar's opening. Wide-mouthed jars are, by far, the best choice because they offer you easy access to the sprouts that will grow inside them. You can get a case (12 jars to a case) of quart-sized, wide-mouth (3-inch diameter) Ball jars for $10 to

$12. Ball jars are a specific kind of jar that are made by the Ball Corporation. They are sturdy and come with the ring/lid tops, which are two-part tops with one section being a flat disc with a rubber washer and the second section being a screw-top ring. For growing sprouts, you can use the ring while the sprouts are germinating and add the lid when you refrigerate post-germination (*lids are covered later in this chapter*).

Aside from the quart-sized, wide-mouth Ball jars, you can use any wide-mouth glass jar that you save from mayonnaise, peanut butter, or grape jelly containers. Of course, the size of the jar will determine the amount of seeds that you will be able to sprout. Keep in mind the larger the jar, the greater your sprouting capabilities.

Other Types of Sprouting Containers

You may wish to experiment with other types of containers similar to jars. There are other methods and types of sprouters that will be covered later in this chapter, but for now we can look at sprouters that are used in a fashion similar to a glass jar.

The most important thing to avoid if you experiment with sprouting containers are containers that are prone to rust. Avoid aluminum, tin, or rust-prone metal of any kind because you want to avoid getting rust in your sprouts. You might choose a clay pot, a discarded plastic gallon-sized pickle jar, or a quart-sized empty yogurt container. You can use just about anything for sprouting. You can grow a garden of sprouts in your bathtub if you so choose. Put a screen in the drain and you are all set with a ready source of water, drainage, and everything you need to grow sprouts for your entire neighborhood.

Strainers and Screens

Whatever you choose to sprout your seeds in, you will need a way to strain/drain the water regularly prior to refreshing the sprout water. A mesh cap will also allow the sprouts to breathe during germination. If you sprout using wide-mouth glass jars, the best way to strain and drain is by purchasing some sprouting strainer lids. These lids are plastic and/or nylon and fit over standard wide-mouth jars. The lids are available through online retailers or stores that sell sprouting equipment and cost between $1.50 and $7. One online retailer you can visit for sprouting materials is WheatgrassKits.com (**www.wheatgrasskits.com**). The advantage to purchasing these lids is that you can get them with different size mesh openings. As your sprouts grow, you can increase the size of the openings, which not only allows for greater circulation, but also accommodates the exit of seed hulls that will run out of the jar or tube as you rinse.

If you do not have lids, you can simply use cheesecloth that is available for about $1 in most grocery stores. **Cheesecloth** is a white, loose-weave cloth fabric that works as a strainer. It is commonly used to make cheese and can also be used for many other activities such as sprouting. If you have the Ball jars with ring tops, you can simply cut a piece of cheesecloth to fit over the mouth of the jar and hold it in place by screwing the ring top over the cheesecloth. Do not use the flat cap section of the ring lid as you want oxygen to get into the jar.

Another material you can use as a strainer/drainer is a piece of nylon screen that is available in most hardware stores. Use the nylon screen in the same way that you use the cheesecloth. Again, you can use just about any non-rusting material as a screen. The advantage that plastic sprouting strainer lids have is that they are easy to clean. If you use cheesecloth or a nylon screen, you will either have to throw it away after each use or you will have to wash it thoroughly.

You can begin your sprouting operation with a jar and a strainer. To get you to consider other methods of sprouting, here are some other types of equipment that can be used to grow sprouts in your home.

Tubes

Sprouting tubes work much the same way that jars do, except for the fact that sprouting tubes have openings on both ends because the tubes have removable tops and bottoms. The tube capacity should be about the same as a 1-quart jar. The advantage to the tube is that it is open on both ends (using plastic screen lids) and allows for better air circulation than a jar does. Tubes should be made of a durable polypropylene or polyethylene plastic. The tubes are used in the same way that jars are. Tubes made specifically for sprouting can be purchased for about $25 each if you can find them at an online retailer. If you buy a tube from a retailer, the retailer will be able to tell you how much the tube holds. *The resource directory in the Appendix will direct you to where you can purchase sprouting tubes.*

It would be much cheaper to make your own tubes with materials easily located at your neighborhood hardware store. To make a tube, simply cut or purchase a clear plastic (polypropylene or polyethylene) section of tube that is about 3 to 4 inches in diameter and about 8 to 10 inches long. You can simply use a rubber band to fasten cheesecloth or a nylon screen to the ends for the strainer. You should be able to make this tube for just a couple of dollars.

Sprout Bags

This item is exactly what it sounds like. Rather than sprouting seeds in a jar, you use a porous material to form a bag used for sprouting. The advantage that the bag has over the jar and/or tube method is it offers the sprouts greater air circulation and is easier to use than the jar. The improved air circulation is due to the fact that the bag allows air to circulate all around the sprouts as opposed to through the singular opening in a jar or two openings in a tube. *Using sprout bags will be explained in detail in Chapter 4.*

The important issue to consider when exploring the sprout bag option is what material to use for a bag. Sprout bags are available for purchase from online retailers, including the website for "Sproutman" Steve Meyerowitz, one of leading proponents of sprouting (**http://sproutman.com**). These sprout bags are generally made of hemp and/or flax. The issues to consider if you make your own bag are strength, breathability, and ability to retain moisture without drying out too quickly.

If you intend on making your own sprout bag, you have to be somewhat handy with a needle and thread or a sewing machine. To make a bag, cut two pieces of your chosen material to rectangular shapes in the size you desire your bag to be. A decent-sized sprout bag is about 7 by 12 inches. Sew the two halves together on three sides of the bag, remembering to reinforce the seams by using double strands of a strong thread or sewing the edges twice. The bag will last longer with reinforced seams. You can create a tunnel for a drawstring around the top, which will make it easier for you to close and hang the bag to drain.

If you are not used to wielding a needle and thread, you can use a square of cloth that is 12 by 12 inches or larger. You will simply place your seeds in the center of the cloth and bring the corners together to form a bag. You can secure the top of the bag (the corners) with a rubber band, shoelace, or piece of string.

You can purchase a sprout bag from an online retailer. *The resources section in the Appendix will tell you where you can get sprout bags.* Hemp/flax sprout bags cost about $12 each.

Sprout Trays

You might decide to use a sprout tray rather than germinating in a jar or a bag. The advantage to sprouting this way is that you are setting the sprouts up in what could be considered a more natural environment for them. The seedlings are spread out and are able to grow similarly to how they would in and on the earth.

You can make a sprout tray out of just about any kind of bamboo basket, plastic colander, or seedling tray purchased at a gardening store. The main issue here is that you allow the tray to drain properly, but not have holes that allow small seeds (like tiny alfalfa seeds) to slip through.

If you choose to construct a tray from a seedling tray you purchase at a gardening store, choose one that is 8 by 10 inches or up to 10 by 20 inches. Use two trays so you can place one tray inside the other for added strength as these trays can be kind of flimsy. You will notice that there are places in the trays that should be pierced for drainage. Use a knife to pierce drainage holes rather than a round utensil because this will protect against seeds plugging the holes. On one end of the tray, slice a lot of holes. You will elevate the other end (the end without the holes) slightly when you sprout and the additional holes will allow for greater drainage.

After you have made your drainage holes, find a clear plastic cover for the tray. You are looking for the kinds of clear plastic covers that you see on grocery store cakes. This will give your tray a greenhouse-like effect. You can also use simple clear plastic wrap for this.

A better alternative to this plastic seedling tray is a bamboo basket. Natural bamboo baskets are perfect for tray sprouters because they drain very easily and they naturally resist the growth of mold. You can purchase 10-inch bamboo baskets for about $6. If you choose to use bamboo, make sure that the basket is natural and free of any paint, shellac, or other coating that may interfere with your health and the health of your sprouts. You can find untreated bamboo baskets at garden stores or just about any large big-box retailer.

If you plan to grow sprouts using soil, you will need a tray that does not drain through the bottom because you will want your soil to retain moisture. There are many kinds of trays you might choose, such as the seedling tray you punctured above, though you will want one that is not punctured. If you are looking for a sturdier tray, cafeteria trays are perfect for this purpose. As you will require an opaque lid for this tray, two cafeteria trays will work perfectly. One tray is used for soil and seed, and the second tray fits nicely on top as a cover.

Commercial and/or Professionally Manufactured Sprouters

If you shop for sprouting equipment in larger health food stores or online, you will come across numerous types of sprouting systems. Many of the sprouting systems you will find at retail outlets are, in some way, versions of the jar, tray, or bag described earlier in this chapter.

Here are some options for commercially made products you can purchase:

- A plastic cup that is similar to a jar with a slotted lid will cost about $15
- Plastic stackable trays cost $15 each or three for $25
- Organic hemp sprouting bags cost about $9
- A three-tiered sprouter costs about $25

(See www.wheatgrasskits.com for more information about these supplies. Also, check the Appendix for a list of retailers.)

Getting into the more professional equipment, you can get an automatic water system barrel sprouter. For about $100, you can purchase a system that automatically delivers a continuous supply of water and air to your sprouts and is easy to expand by adding additional barrels.

Beyond the equipment described on the pages here, you may come across other types of sprouting systems as you do research into the world of sprouting, and you may even develop your own system. As you begin, however, you will probably start with the jar (or some variation of the jar), the bag, or the tray to use for sprouting. These are all reliable and acceptable ways of starting your foray into growing healthy sprouts.

No matter which system you choose, keep your equipment clean. If you use glass jars or any plastic containers or jar, wash them well in hot water with a good detergent. Be sure to rinse the detergent thoroughly from your equipment after washing. If you use bags to germinate your sprouts, turn the bags inside out and wash them well in hot water with detergent. Turning them inside out ensures you get all the little sprouts that may have stuck to the inside of the bag when you emptied it. After you wash the bag, rinse it out in a water and hydrogen peroxide solution. Follow the directions on the hydrogen peroxide for the amount you use with water. If you are using a food grade (35 percent) hydrogen peroxide, you can use it at full strength. If you are using 100 percent hydrogen peroxide, you should dilute it with three parts water to one part hydrogen peroxide.

Soil

This is not equipment per se, but it is necessary for those of you who care to take your growing past the sprout stage. You may find that once you establish a knack for growing sprouts and you enjoy all the health benefits, as well as the taste of sprouts, you will want to establish a small indoor garden to grow wheatgrass, sunflower greens, buckwheat lettuce, or pea greens. Grains such as wheat and greens such as sunflowers make wonderful sprouts that can be used in many recipes, but when you allow the seeds to mature a little longer, there are additional uses and benefits these seeds can offer. The reason that soil becomes necessary is that the sprouts listed above demand a slightly longer growth time, and after five or six days the seeds exhaust their stored fuel supply. Offering these tiny beings soil, a little more water, and a look at the sun gives them the nutrients they require to grow a little more.

The dirt from your yard probably will not do for your little sprouts because most yard dirt is hard, full of clay, and lacks the nutrients that your sprouts will desire. To encourage your little charges to grow and be happy, you will need to offer them soil that is light and airy. The best recipe for success will be a mixture of potting soil and peat moss or vermiculite, which is a mineral commonly used in gardening that expands in heat. The mixture should be one part to one part. After mixing the soil and peat moss or vermiculite, you can use a tray as described earlier in this chapter as your garden. *Directions for growing a variety of greens will be given in Chapter 5.*

Greenhouses

If you choose to grow using soil, there may come a time when you will want to employ a greenhouse. Greenhouses can come in many different shapes and styles. Like growing in any other medium that has been described in this chapter, you can choose to construct your own greenhouse or purchase one from a retailer.

If you choose to construct a greenhouse, make sure you enclose your garden completely in a clear bubble. A simple plastic wrapping can work for this, but it is better to construct a larger area that will provide more circulation. This is easily accomplished with several coat hangers and heavy-duty plastic wrap. Your goal is simply to surround your basket of sprouts in a clear bubble; it is not necessary that the tent is air-tight.

If you choose to purchase a greenhouse that you can use in your home or apartment, you can buy them starting at about $40. *See the Appendix for information on where to find this product.*

Making an indoor greenhouse

There are simple instructions that describe a way of putting together a basic indoor greenhouse for a single plant, but with a little imagination and very little cost, you can make an indoor greenhouse that will allow you to accommodate numerous plants.

There is always the option of purchasing an indoor greenhouse and greenhouse supplies. If you would like to consider this option, check out the mini-greenhouses at **http://www.hydrofarm.com.**

If you are handy and would rather build it yourself, you can make it with things that you already have around the house or that are easily available at your local hardware store or supermarket.

You simply need to provide a frame of some sort and a way to enclose the frame in such a way that sunlight gets in. For a frame, you might consider an open shelving unit (such as utility shelves) or a table (such as a card table) turned upside down. You can enclose the frame with a clear plastic shower curtain or two. The plastic covering can be secured with tacks, clothespins, or any other device that allows for easy manipulation.

When you enclose the frame, be sure that you arrange an easy access to your greenhouse as you will need to water and care for your plants. Access means being able to open the enclosed space to regulate, to some degree, the temperature. (To monitor the temperature, place a thermometer in the middle of the greenhouse in a place that is easily visible.) The greenhouse is placed in a location in your home or apartment that allows for maximum sunlight.

There are a number of greenhouse plans available online that describe more elaborate set-ups with grow lights and heaters. These more elaborate greenhouses are a little more difficult to build but give you greater ability to control the greenhouse environment.

When it comes to planning to your sprouts, choose a method and experiment with it. Try another and see how you like it. You will find that no matter which method you choose or what equipment you decide upon, sprouting is easy and relatively inexpensive. Before you run out and purchase a $100 sprouter, see how easy it is to make your own. Like most people who grow sprouts, you will probably find that growing sprouts in a jar or a simple bag is the easiest and most economical way to go.

Now that you have an idea as to what you might need to get started growing sprouts, it is time to explore what seeds you can consider growing.

CASE STUDY: EVRETT LUNQUIST AND RUTH CHANTRY

Evrett Lunquist
and Ruth Chantry
Common Good Farm
www.commongoodfarm.com

Common Good Farm is a Community Supported Agriculture (CSA) farm just outside of Lincoln, Nebraska. Evrett Lunquist said a mason jar with a regularly rinsed screen that is placed upside down is the best way for a home sprouter to get started. He said multi-tier racks may be more practical for sprouters who are growing multiple stages of sprouts at once.

He believes that the easiest seeds to sprout are alfalfa, mung, and brassica because everything is contained and only water is used. He thinks that the most difficult sprouts are peas and sunflowers because soil and a tray with drainage are required.

Lunquist said important item to consider before purchasing seeds to sprout is whether to choose organic seeds. "A seed should only be used if it processed for human consumption. Organic seed is raised according to the National Organic Program standards that prohibit the use of most synthetic substances and limit the use of manure to prevent contact with food prior to food harvest."

He said the best thing beginning sprouters can do is buy a good book as a reference guide and keep the sprouts cool and well rinsed to prevent mold from growing.

Chapter 3

What to Sprout

The range of seeds, grain, legumes, and nuts that are available for sprouting is extensive. As you begin to think about what to sprout, it is best to go with what you know. Most people have had and enjoy alfalfa sprouts on sandwiches and bean sprouts (probably mung bean sprouts) in Asian stir-fry dishes. A few more may have enjoyed sprouted wheat in a loaf of bread or broccoli sprouts in a salad. This chapter is devoted to digging deep into the variety of seeds, grains, legumes, and nuts that can be grown in a home sprouting station. The list of these items is long with each item having its own special taste and nutritional value.

This chapter will also discuss toxins in seeds, grains, legumes, and nuts. It will explore those items that you should avoid and why. The chapter will dismiss some myths about the toxicity of some kinds of seeds and beans. The toxicity of raw beans will be discussed as the book looks at the variety of ways to sprout and cook beans such as soy, garbanzo, and kidney beans. Also, this chapter will examine the topic of the toxicity of fruit seeds, especially apple seeds, and dispel the myth of the high levels of cyanide in apple seeds.

Choosing Your Seeds

Before you get into the list of types of seeds you might consider sprouting, take a moment to consider what is important about those seeds. When you look to buy any type of seed for sprouting, make sure that you are buying organic or natural seeds. As described in Chapters 1 and 2, seeds are a great source of energy and materials they received from their mother plant. If these seeds are derived from a plant that was treated with pesticides, herbicides, and other chemicals, those chemicals were passed on to the seeds. Be sure that the seeds you purchase for sprouting and consuming are certified organic or come from a natural source you can have faith in. *Check the Appendix for a directory of seed sources.*

The following list of sprout suggestions is by no means a complete one. There are hundreds of seeds that might fall into the category of those that are sproutable and beneficial to the human diet. This list reflects seeds that are among the most commonly sprouted and are readily available as organic seeds at natural food grocers or through online resources.

Another word about the following list: The health benefits noted are not complete and there are health benefits to sprouts beyond the normal list of vitamins, minerals, protein, and dietary fiber. As noted in Chapter 1, sprouts such as broccoli contain compounds such as sulforaphane that have been shown to have cancer-fighting properties. Many sprouts contain a variety of phenolic compounds that have been shown to have many health benefits to the consumer. **Phenolic compounds** are chemical compounds that are essential to the growth of plants and have been shown to have a wide array of health benefits to humans. Among the claims made related to these compounds are cholesterol-fighting properties, protection against coronary heart disease, and cancer-preventing abilities.

The nutritional information listed below has been collected from the U.S. Department of Agriculture (USDA) Agriculture Research Service Nutrient Data Laboratory. The stated nutrition facts are for raw sprouted items. The nutrient data for items is altered to some degree by processes such as baking and cooking. For further information on the nutritional content of the listed items, as well as the nutritional content of hundreds of other items, refer to **www.nal.usda.gov/fnic/foodcomp/search**. At this site, you will be able to type in the kind of food you are interested in getting nutrition facts about and the site will offer you a great deal of information related to suggested serving sizes, calories, and the nutritional benefits of the items.

Variey	Nutrition Facts	Serving Suggestions
Adzuki bean	*Rich in protein, amino acids, iron, niacin, and calcium*	*Stir-fry, casseroles, salads, sandwiches, breads*
Alfafa	*Rich in vitamins C, and B6, riboflavin, folate, magnesium, phosphorus, zinc, copper, manganese, protein, thiamin, pantothenic acid, calcium, and iron*	*Juices, salads, sandwiches, breads*
Almond	*Extrememly high in protein. Also rich in calcium, potassium, and amino acids*	*Breads, desserts, drinks, salads, snacks*
Amaranth	*High in iron magnesium phosphorus, and potassium*	*Breads, cakes, cereals, soups*
Arugula	*Very high in protein, vitamin B6, amino acids, iron and calcium*	*Pasta, salads, sandwiches*
Barley	*High in protein, iron, zinc, phosphorus, and calcium*	*Breads, cereals, salads, snacks, soups*
Black turtle bean	*High in protein, iron, zinc, phosporus, and calcium*	*Breads, casseroles, dips, salads, soups, stir-fry*

Variety	Nutrition Facts	Serving Suggestions
Broccoli	Rich in vitamins K, C, B6, and E, folate, dietary fiber phosphorus, potassium, and magnesium	Salads, sandwiches, soups
Buckwheat	Good source of vitamin B6, iron, calcium, magnesium, and essential amino acids	Baked goods, cereals, sandwiches, salads, snacks
Cabbage	Provides vitamins B6, C, E, folate, calcium, iron, potassium, and phosphorus	Salads, sandwices, soups
Chickpea (also called garbanzo bean)	Rich in vitamin B6, protein, folate, potassium, iron, manganese, copper, zinc, and calcium	Stir-fry, casseroles, salads, sandwiches, breads
Chive	High in vitamins C and B6, riboflavin, folate, calcium, iron, magnesium, potassium, copper, manganese, thiamin, niacin, pantothenic acid, phosphorus, and zinc	Casseroles, sandwiches, salads
Fenugreek	Vitamins B6 and C, calcium, iron, magnesium, phosphorus, potassium, and zinc	Casseroles, curries, salads, soups
Green pea	Good source of vitamin C and B6, thiamin, magnesium, phosphorus, copper, manganese, and an excellent source of potassium	Casseroles, dips, dressings, salads, soups, stir-fry
Lentil	An excellent source of folate and manganese, and a good source of thiamin, iron, phosphorus, and copper	Breads, casseroles, curries, salads, soups
Lettuce	Good source of potassium and zinc	Salads, sandwiches
Millet	Good source of calcium, iron, magnesium, pantothenic acid, potassium, amino acids, and protein	Breads, cereals, casseroles, salads

Variety	Nutrition Facts	Serving Suggestions
Mung bean	Great source of protein and a very good source of vitamins B6 and C, calcium, iron, magnesium, potassium, and amino acids	Stir-fry, casseroles, salads, sandwiches, breads
Mustard seed	A powerhouse of protein and a great source of vitamins A, B6, and C, calcium, iron, magnesium, phosphorus, potassium, and zinc	Casseroles, dips, dressings, sandwiches, salads, soups
Oats	An excellent source of protein, calcium, iron, magnesium, phosphorus, potassium, and amino acids	Breads, cereals, salads, sandwiches, snacks
Onion	Excellent source of protein, and a good source of vitamins C and B6, calcium, iron, magnesium, phosphorus, potassium, and zinc	Casseroles, dips, dressings, sandwiches, salads, soups
Peanuts	Excellent source of protein, vitamin B6, calcium, iron, magnesium, niacin, phosphorus, potassium, and amino acids	Breads, casseroles, salads, sandwiches, snacks, stir-fry
Pumpkin	Great source of amino acids	Breads, cereals, smoothies, snacks
Quinoa	Contains protein, vitamins A, B6, E, calcium, iron, magnesium, niacin, phosphorus, and potassium	Breads, cereals, salads, sandwiches
Radish	Great protein source and a very good source of vitamins A, B6, C, calcium, iron, magnesium, phosphorus, potassium, and zinc	Sandwiches, salads
Rye	Good source of protein, vitamin C, calcium, iron, magnesium, phosphorus, and an excellent source of dietary fiber	Breads, cereals, salads, soups
Sesame	Good source of protein, vitamins A and C, calcium, iron, magnesium, amino acids, and an excellent source of phosphorus	Breads, cereals, salads, soups
Soybean	Excellent source of protein, vitamins A, B6, and C, calcium, iron, and phosphorus	Breads, casseroles, salads, stir-fry

Variety	Nutrition Facts	Serving Suggestions
Sunflower	Great source of protein and an excellent source of vitamins B6, and E, calcium, iron, magnesium, niacin, phosphorus, potassium, and dietary fiber	Breads, cereals, salads, snacks, soups
Wheat	A good source of protein, vitamins C and B6, calcium, iron, magnesium, pantothenic acid, phosphorus, and amino acids	Breads, cereals, salads, snacks, soups

Something not mentioned in the list above is how each of these sprouts tastes. You can count on them tasting somewhat similar to the plant they will grow into, though sometimes they will taste more intense or milder as variations will occur with seeds. Taste will be affected by the length of time you sprout the seed. Some seeds will grow blander as they age while others will increase in potency. Beyond all the variables that will affect the taste is your personal preference. If you have not tasted a particular item, experiment with it. It is impossible to describe a specific taste to someone who has not tasted it for him or herself. There is an old saying that you cannot describe how a peach tastes to someone who has never eaten one. Know, then, that a radish sprout will taste like a radish, but different. Black bean sprouts will taste like black beans, but somewhat different. Do not be afraid to experiment, grow, and taste new experiences.

Toxic Sprouts?

While growing sprouts at home presents nothing for you to be afraid of if you keep your equipment clean and follow all the safety procedures you normally follow in preparing any food, there are persistent attacks on sprouts as dangerous foods. Many of these warnings stem from the notion that a number of beans and seeds contain toxins that present a health hazard.

Peas have been a subject of concern in some circles for containing a toxin known as lathyrogen. Lathyrogen causes a condition known as **lathyrism**, a paralysis of the lower extremities. The fact is there is a variety of pea that does contain this toxin, but the variety in question is an inedible, ornamental breed. This type of pea is not available as a food source. The peas that are consumed as a normal part of the human diet do not contain this toxin.

Another toxin that is often the subject of concern is **canavanine**. Canavanine is believed to cause kidney failure and exacerbate the symptoms of lupus. Trace amounts of canavanine are found in alfalfa sprouts. However, to get the amount of this toxin from alfalfa sprouts that might have an ill effect on one's health would mean eating huge amounts of sprouts every day for a year. A generous helping of alfala sprouts might give you 2 to 3 milligrams of canavanine, but you must consume 14,000 milligrams of canavanine to experience the toxic effects. In other words, you would have to eat about 7,000 servings on alfalfa sprouts in a 24-hour period. That said, you must also remember that large amounts of vitamin A and a number of trace minerals are also toxic when eaten in large amounts regularly. A standard multivitamin has 3,500 IU of vitamin A. Approximately three carrots have about 34,000 IU of vitamin A. However, a toxic level of vitamin A is considered to be about 200,000 IU taken over a long period of time.

You should pay particular attention to large beans (kidney or lima) when and if you decide to sprout them, as many large beans contain substances called enzyme inhibitors. If left uncooked, these enzyme inhibitors make proper digestion difficult, which can result in flatulence and a certain amount of digestive discomfort. Therefore, large beans should be cooked after sprouting and prior to consuming. Some of these beans and their sprouts taste bad if eaten raw and can present digestive issues. Cooking the beans properly destroys these enzyme inhibitors. Kidney beans can be properly cooked for consumption with as little as ten minutes of boiling. Cooking them for any shorter than that will give you a hard bean that tastes bad, which you would not want to eat anyway. *Directions for cooking bean sprouts can be found in Chapter 11.*

The chart above lists the almond as a sproutable seed with numerous health benefits. On the other hand, it is rumored that almonds contain lethal amounts of cyanide, which is a toxin that causes many human ills when taken in lethal amounts. Again, there is not enough cyanide in almonds to harm you. You would have to eat several hundred pounds of them in one sitting to take in that much cyanide. Given that, you would probably die of other causes before the cyanide got you. Other plants and seeds that contain trace amounts of cyanide are apple seeds, lima beans, and tapioca. Like canavanine, vitamin A, or iron, you are more likely to receive the health benefits from eating almonds than you are to be poisoned by eating them. Feel free to sprout and snack away.

CASE STUDY: BOB SANDERSON

Bob Sanderson
Jonathan's Sprouts, Inc.
www.jonathansorganic.com

Bob Sanderson is the co-founder and co-owner of Jonathan's Sprouts, Inc. He has been growing and selling sprouts for 34 years.

Growing sprouts commercially offers Sanderson the pleasure of being a part of a small, committed community that does productive work and helps provide fresh, nutritious food to others. Sanderson said, "When [the sprouts] are fresh, they are the freshest, healthiest food on earth."

Sanderson said he does not know of any edible seeds to avoid sprouting, but it is likely that seeds produce protective chemicals during the sprouting stage that can be toxic in concentrated amounts. Consuming these chemicals in small amounts can be very beneficial. He said this value is greater in organic seeds compared to conventional seeds because conventional seeds are covered with pesticides.

"Some people are proposing that 'conventional' is less risky than organic," Sanderson said. "I think the underlying issue is the extent to which one trusts nature versus chemical companies."

When asked his favorite ways to use sprouts, he said, "They are good in salads, sandwiches, and stir-fries."

Seed Costs

Another issue not indicated on the chart above is the cost of seeds. As you might imagine, the range of costs is great and depends on type of seed, availability, location, time of year, and a number of other factors. As you shop for seeds, you should look for seeds that are organic and produced as close to your home as possible because this means that the seeds have not been treated with any unwanted chemicals and are relatively fresh. Seeds do have a long shelf life, averaging about two to four years, but you are more likely to get viable seeds from stock that has not been sitting on a shelf or in a bin somewhere for a long time.

As you consider the per pound price of any of the seeds listed below, remember that the weight will multiply from two to ten times when you sprout the seeds. From 3 tablespoons of alfalfa seeds you will get 3 to 4 cups of sprouts, and from 2 tablespoons of broccoli seeds you will get 2 cups of sprouts. This is an important factor to keep in mind as you consider the economics of sprouting and the cost of seeds.

An example of what you might expect to pay for several types of seeds is detailed here. The prices given are for organic seeds for sprouting according to a variety of online seed retailers.

- Adzuki: $6 to $10 per lb.
- Alfalfa: $7.50 to $8.50 per lb.
- Almond: $17 to $20 per lb.
- Amaranth: $6 to $9 per lb.
- Arugula: $16 to $20 per lb.
- Barley (unhulled): $5 to $7 per lb.
- Black turtle bean: $5 to $7 per lb.
- Broccoli: $25 per lb.
- Buckwheat (hulled): $5 to $7 per lb.
- Cabbage: $7 to $25 per lb.
- Chickpea (garbanzo): $6 to $8 per lb.
- Chive: $20 per ½ lb.
- Clover: $7 to $15 per lb.
- Fenugreek: $7 to $10 per lb.
- Green Pea: $3 to $7 per lb.
- Lentil: $6 to $8 per lb.
- Lettuce: $6 to $60 per ¼ lb.
- Millet: $4 to $8 per lb.
- Mung bean: $5 to $7 per lb.
- Mustard seed: $8 to $12 per lb.
- Oats: $5 to $7 per lb.
- Onion: $20 to $25 per ½ lb.
- Peanuts: $8 to $12 per lb.
- Pumpkin: $12 to $16 per lb.
- Quinoa: $7 to $10 per lb.
- Radish: $8 to $12 per lb.
- Rye: $4 to $8 per lb.
- Sesame: $6 to $10 per lb.
- Soybean: $4 to $8 per lb.
- Sunflower: $6 to $10 per lb.
- Wheat: $2.50 to $3.50 per lb.

You will note that some of the grains listed above are hulled or unhulled. The **hull** of a grain is the hard, inedible, protective outer layer. Hulled grain has had this outer layer removed, while unhulled grain has the outer layer intact. Hulled barley will not sprout, but hulled buckwheat will sprout.

You might also note the large price range of lettuce seed. There are many types of lettuce that are available for growing. The types range from a simple iceberg lettuce to the fancier types such as the Yugoslavian Red Butterhead.

The first place to look for any of the above seeds is at a local health food store that deals primarily in locally grown produce. Better yet, if you know any farmers that grow any of the items you are interested in sprouting, talk to them and buy directly from the farmer. Beyond those two suggestions, there are a number of very reputable mail-order retailers that are listed in the Appendix of this book. Two examples of great sources of seeds are Wood Prairie Farm (**www.woodprairie.com**) and WheatgrassKits.com (**www.wheatgrasskits.com/**).

Growing Organic

The importance of choosing organic seeds cannot be stressed enough. If you recall the description of a seed's anatomy and life cycle in Chapter 1, you will remember that plants store everything they receive from their environment in each and every seed they produce. The health of the flower is the health of the seed, which means that they also pass the toxins such as herbicides, pesticides, and growth regulators on to their seeds.

If you choose seeds that are certified organic, you are getting a product that is grown without chemicals used to control insects, weeds, and growth. Organic farmers control these issues through natural means. Insects are controlled using predatory insects that do not harm their crops. Chickens and other animals are also used to control insects. Weeds are controlled through crop rotation and are also picked by hand instead of using pesticides. Certified organic also is insurance that the seeds you choose have not been genetically modified. **Genetically modified seeds** are seeds that have been changed to ensure things like higher crop yield and root strength.

The bottom line for you, the seed sprouter, is that you have viable seeds that are clean and free of chemicals and have been produced in an environmentally friendly manner. Read labels before you buy. Again, if you can, buy direct from the farmer. If you cannot buy from the farmer, make sure that your seeds are certified organic.

An exception to the certified organic suggestion is to buy seeds from small farmers that are grown naturally. Some small farms and growers are just too small to go through the process of having their farm certified organic; however, this does not mean that they do not or cannot grow organic produce. If the small farm is not certified organic, talk to the farmer or the retailer to get as much information as you can about the seeds you are buying. Remember, you are going to be eating these seeds and feeding them to your family. One of the main selling points of growing and consuming sprouts is that you know what you are eating and where it came from.

Storing Seeds

When you purchase seeds, you will probably buy more than you can sprout in a single batch. For example, you will probably buy more than 3 tablespoons of alfalfa seeds. Depending on where you purchase your seeds, you will probably purchase between 2 ounces and 1 pound. This brings up the issue of storage. What do you do with 1 pound of alfalfa seeds you purchased that you are not ready to use yet?

Glass Jars

The simplest manner of storage is that same glass canning jar you use to sprout. The difference here is that you do not necessarily have to use a wide-mouth jar, and you will use a solid lid as opposed to a screen. Canning jars come with ring lids and tops that have rubber gaskets at the edge to make a good seal. The important factors to keep in mind if you choose to use a glass jar for storage are cleanliness and the jar's seal. The best way to make sure your jar is clean is to sterilize it. To sterilize a glass jar, simply place a canning jar and lid in boiling water for five minutes.

After you have sterilized the jar, it is important that the jar is completely dry before you fill it with seeds. To provide a double amount of sterilization insurance, you can dry your jars in a 200-degree oven. This will dry the jar and sterilize it. Alternatively, you can just allow your jars to air dry. The point is, make sure they are completely dry or you may end up with moldy seeds.

After the jars are dry (and cooled), place your seeds in the jars and tightly seal them. Store them in a cool, dry place in your house. A dark location is better than a light location. Remember, light, moisture, and warmth are what trigger a seed's activity. Thus, by storing them in dark, dry, and cool places, you are ensuring the seeds remain dormant.

Using buckets

If you have larger amounts of seeds that are difficult for jars to accommodate, you can choose to store them in large buckets. Sterilization and sealing is every bit as important with buckets as it is with jars. Make sure your buckets are clean and have rubber gaskets on the lid to seal. You can find a complete line of food storage buckets at **https://www.usaemergencysupply.com/emergency_supplies/food_storage_equipment.htm**.

Plastic bags

Other methods of storage that are acceptable, though not as effective as glass jars, are plastic storage bags. If you choose to use plastic bags to store your seeds, it is recommended that you double-bag the seeds, make them as vacuum-packed as possible, and not store seeds in this manner for longer than three months because plastic bags are easier for pests to get into than glass or hard plastic.

The four important things to remember as you put your seeds away for storage are to keep them dry, cool, and away from sunlight and pests. If you can accomplish these things, you should be able store most seeds for two to five years if you keep them at room temperature (70 degrees).

Freezing seeds

If you have room in your freezer, freezing seeds is a perfectly acceptable way to store seeds. The advantage to storing seeds in the freezer is that the freeze will kill any pests that may be in your seeds, which is a problem that sprouters occasionally encounter. Sometimes the pests will be on the seed and sometimes the pests will actually be in the seeds. This is an issue that should not alarm you because, whether you aware of it or not, all foods face similar problems and issues, especially natural, unprocessed foods such as seeds. The bugs are not harmful to you and if you deal with your seeds properly, you will not have them hatching and flying around your house.

The best way to deal with the problem of pests on seeds is to freeze the seeds for 48 hours. The freeze kills any bug or egg that may have landed on your seeds. Place the seed in a doubled plastic bag and place it in the freezer. Double bagging will protect it from freezer burn. After the freeze, you can continue to keep the seeds in the freezer or you can transfer them to jars or buckets.

If you buy large amounts of seeds that will not fit into your freezer, make sure that the seeds remain in a sealed container until you are ready to use them. If you keep that sealed container at 65 degrees or cooler, you will most likely not have to worry about any pest hatchings.

Deciding What Sprout to Grow

The biggest determining factor to consider as you decide what to sprout should be the taste preferences of you and your family. Toxins and pests aside, any seed or seeds you decide to sprout will provide you with great health benefits. The ease of growing, low cost, and variety of vitamins, minerals, and other essential dietary requirements sprouts offer make this a food that is extremely healthy, highly economical, and exceedingly convenient.

As you decide which seeds to start with, go with what you know. For example, alfalfa sprouts are quite common and easy to grow. As you learn the variety of sprouting techniques in the following chapter, do not be afraid to experiment with new methods and taste experiences. You will find your experiments to be rewarding on many different levels.

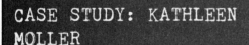

CASE STUDY: KATHLEEN
MOLLER

Kathleen Moller
WheatgrassKits.com
www.wheatgrasskits.com

Kathleen Moller has been growing sprouts for about 20 years. Her company, WheatgrassKits.com, has been in business for more than ten years. They are the No. 1 wheatgrass destination online and have more than 85,000 customers.

Moller reports that she enjoys sprouts "for their crunchy taste and because they have enzymes to help with digestion. There is a life force in sprouts: enzymes. I believe the life force transfers to the life force of the human body, thus giving more energy."

She said that she thinks the best method for home sprouters is a product called the Handy Pantry Sprout garden. "I get consistently good sprouts every time from this sprouter and one can sprout volumes or just a little. It has three layers."

Moller feels that broccoli is the hardest seed to sprout. "It seems to grow slowly and prefers to sprout in glass rather than plastic. Mung bean and fenugreek seem to be the easiest for me to sprout. I get excellent sprouts in about three days from both." Chia and flax are special seeds that must be sprouted in a terra cotta dish, sprinkled on the dry dish, immersed in water and covered. The seeds will draw the water from many seeds that she has not yet sprouted, but she has not avoided any yet. For those new to sprouting, Moller advised, "Try many different ways to sprout. Refrigerate after about three to four days and the sprouts will continue to grow in the fridge, although more slowly. Water about every third day after refrigerating."

As far as ways to enjoy your sprouts, Moller offers this suggestion: "Sprout a mixture of peas, adzuki beans, lentils, and mung beans. Mix the sprouts with chopped red pepper, tomatoes, onions, and celery. Sprinkle with your favorite salad dressing and add black or green olives. You can also blend this and serve as a loaf. Drizzle dressing on top."

Chapter 4

How to Sprout

"So never lose an opportunity of urging a practical beginning, however small, for it is wonderful how often in such matters the mustard seed germinates and roots itself."

——Florence Nightingale, nurse/humanitarian

This chapter will describe the variety of methods you might employ to sprout seeds. This is where the equipment described in Chapter 2 will meet the seeds described in Chapter 3. The chapter will begin by giving general explanations as to how to employ each method and then outline specific instructions on how to sprout each of the seeds described in Chapter 3. Prior to beginning any of the operations listed below, be sure that you have a clean working environment, clean equipment, and clean hands. Doing all you can do to avoid contaminating your sprouts should always be the first step you take, no matter what sprouting method you choose to follow.

Another good practice to follow, no matter which method of sprouting you choose, is to taste your sprouts at each rinse. You will note in the sprouting instructions chart that there is a recommended sprouting time. As you grow your sprouts, when you taste them with each rinsing, you will note slight changes in flavor. As you taste your sprouts, note the point at which you find a preferable taste and let your taste be your guide as to when your sprouting is complete.

No matter which method of sprouting you choose, you will be surprised at what a simple wonder sprouting is. If you have children, allow them to become involved every step of the way, from rinsing the seeds to harvesting the sprouts. Assisting in and watching the progression from seed to sprout to table is a simple marvel to behold.

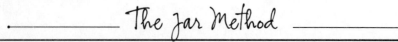

The Jar Method

Using a jar to sprout seeds is the simplest and most commonly used method of growing sprouts because the equipment is readily available and it is an easy technique to follow. While growing sprouts in a jar is not the best method for all types of seeds, it is a perfectly good way to get started growing most seeds.

Necessities

- Large, wide-mouth jar(s) (quart-sized jars are a good place to start)
- Screens (cheesecloth, plastic, or a nylon screen for the top of the jars)
- Measuring spoons
- Sieve
- Organic sprouting seeds (*The suggested amount of seeds are indicated on the chart shown later in this chapter*)
- Water (If you live in a place with clean and reliable drinking tap water, using it is perfectly fine. If you should not drink your tap water, use bottled drinking water.)

Procedure

1. Examine seeds to be sprouted, discarding any discolored seeds, hulls, broken seeds, or any foreign matter.

2. Place the seeds in a small bowl and cover them with water.

3. Allow the seeds to sit in the water for ten minutes.

4. Pour the seeds and water from the bowl into a sieve.

5. Run cool water over the seeds in the sieve to clean them.

6. Place seeds in wide-mouth jar.

7. Cover the top of the jar with plastic strainer top (you can also use cheesecloth or any top that will allow the sprouting seeds to breathe and can be used as a strainer.)

8. Add cool water to jar. (A good rule of thumb is that you add four times the amount of water as the amount of seeds.)

9. Soak the seeds according to the soaking time indicated in the sprouting instructions chart.

10. Pour the water off through the strainer top, leaving the seeds in the jar. As you pour the water off, swirl the seeds around in the jar.

11. Allow the jar to rest in a cool, dark place at a 45 degree angle with the top facing down to allow the excess water to drain off. Make sure that the seeds do not completely cover the opening in the strainer.

12. Rinse and drain the sprouts three times a day for the recommended sprouting time indicated in the sprouting instructions chart.

13. Each time you rinse and drain the seeds, swirl the water in the jar to move the sprouting seeds around.

14. After you rinse and drain, allow the jar to rest in a cool, dark place at a 45-degree angle with the top facing down to allow the excess water to drain off. Make sure that the seeds do not completely cover the opening in the strainer.

15. After the seeds have sprouted according to the sprouting time indicated in the sprouting instructions chart, expose them to indirect sunlight for a day or two until small green leaves appear. (Some sprouts do not require this step. These sprouts will be noted in the sprouting instructions chart.) Do not expose the sprouts to direct

sunlight as it is too harsh for them.

16. After the seeds are fully sprouted and the leaves appear, place the sprouts in a bowl of cool water and swirl them around with a clean hand. This action will remove hulls that will float to the top of the water. Scoop the hulls out with your hand or with a spoon.

17. Drain the sprouts.

18. Allow the sprouts to dry for at least eight hours before you refrigerate them. Drying them will help to protect against spoilage and mold and refrigeration will keep your sprouts crisp and fresh.

19. Store the sprouts in the refrigerator for up to ten days, though they are best eaten as soon as possible.

The Tube Method

Sprouting seeds using a tube is nearly identical to using a jar. The advantage to sprouting with a tube is that you have two open ends that allow for greater air circulation.

Necessities

- Tube for sprouting (*see tube description in Chapter 2*)
- Screens (cheesecloth, plastic, or nylon screen for the top of the jars)
- Solid cap (This cap should allow you to fill the tube with water and not leak.)
- Measuring spoons
- Sieve
- Organic sprouting seeds (*The suggested amount of seeds are indicated on the chart shown later in this chapter*)
- Water (If you live in a place with clean and reliable drinking tap water, using it is perfectly fine. If you should not drink your tap water, use bottled drinking water.)

Procedure

1. Examine seeds to be sprouted, discarding any discolored seeds, hulls, broken seeds, or any foreign matter.

2. Place the seeds in a small bowl and cover them with water.

3. Allow the seeds to sit in the water for ten minutes.

4. Pour the seeds and water from the bowl into a sieve.

5. Run cool water over the seeds in the sieve to clean them.

6. Place a solid cap on one end of the tube.

7. Place seeds in tube.

8. Cover the top of the tube with plastic strainer top. (You can also use cheesecloth or any top that will allow the sprouting seeds to breathe and be used as a strainer.)

9. Add cool water to tube. (A good rule of thumb is that you add four times the amount of water as the amount of seeds.)

10. Soak the seeds according to the soaking time indicated in the sprouting instructions chart.

11. Pour the water off through the strainer top, leaving the seeds in the tube. As you pour the water off, swirl the seeds around in the tube.

12. Replace the solid cap with a strainer cap. You should now have a strainer cap on each end of the tube.

13. Allow the tube to rest in a cool, dark place at a 45-degree angle that allows the excess water to drain off through one end of the tube. Make sure that the seeds do not completely cover the opening in the strainer.

14. Rinse and drain the sprouts three times a day for the recommended sprouting time indicated in the sprouting instructions chart. This can be accomplished in several ways. You can place the solid cap on one end of the tube, fill the tube with water, and then drain it, replacing the solid cap with a strainer cap when you have drained the water. An alternative method is to run water through the tube that will immediately run out of the bottom of the tube. If you choose this method, it

is best to run the water through the tube using a spray nozzle because the spray nozzle will spread out the flow of water and is not as hard on the sprouts.

15. After the seeds are fully sprouted and the leaves appear, place the sprouts in a bowl of cool water and swirl them around with a clean hand. This action will remove hulls that will float to the top of the water. Scoop the hulls out with your hand or with a spoon.

16. Drain the sprouts.

17. Allow the sprouts to dry for at least eight hours before you refrigerate them.

18. Store the sprouts in the refrigerator for up to ten days, though they are best eaten as soon as possible.

The Bag Method

Growing sprouts in a bag is a method of sprouting that is gaining popularity. Once you have the bag that works well for you, the method is simpler and less cumbersome than the already simple jar method.

Necessities
- Jar (optional)
- Bag for sprouting (see bag description in Chapter 2)
- Measuring spoons
- Sieve
- Organic sprouting seeds (The suggested amount of seeds are indicated on the chart shown later in this chapter.)
- Water (If you live in a place with clean and reliable drinking tap water, using it is perfectly fine. If you should not drink your tap water, use bottled drinking water.)
- Plastic bag with holes punched for ventilation (The bag should be large enough to accommodate your sprout bag.)

Procedure

1. Examine seeds to be sprouted, discarding any discolored seeds, hulls, broken seeds, or any foreign matter.

2. Place the seeds in a small bowl and cover them with water.

3. Allow the seeds to sit in the water for ten minutes.

4. Pour the seeds and water from the bowl into a sieve.

5. Run cool water over the seeds in the sieve to clean them.

6. (Optional Step) You can choose to do your initial soaking in a jar. If so, place seeds in wide-mouth jar. (Note: You can also place the seeds in your bag and place your bag in the jar of water, which alleviates the need for steps 7 and 10.)

7. Cover the top of the jar with plastic strainer top. (You can also use cheesecloth or any top that will allow the sprouting seeds to breathe and be used as a strainer.)

8. Add cool water to your jar. (A good rule of thumb is that you add four times the amount of water as the amount of seeds.)

9. Soak the seeds according to the soaking time indicated in the sprouting instructions chart. (Whether you choose to soak the seeds in the bag or in a jar, the main point is that you need to initially soak the seeds according to the soaking time indicated in the sprouting instructions.)

10. Pour the water off through the strainer top, leaving the seeds in the jar. As you pour the water off, swirl the seeds around in the jar or use the bag as a sieve and pour seeds and water out of the jar into the sprouting bag.

11. Place seeds in sprouting bag.

12. Dip the bag of soaked seeds in a bowl of water to moisten the bag.

13. Hang the bag to drain for 15 minutes. You can hang the bag over your sink or over a bowl.

14. Place the sprouting bag inside the plastic bag, which helps the bag of

seed retain some moisture.

15. Hang the bag over your sink or a bowl.

16. Rinse and drain the sprouts three times a day for the recommended sprouting time indicated in the sprouting instructions chart. This can be accomplished in several ways. The first way you can do this is to remove the sprout bag from the plastic bag. You can place the sprout bag in a bowl of water and very gently massage the bag, which moves water up in the bag's weave. An alternative method is to run water over the seeds as you gently massage the bag. If you choose this method, it is best to run the water through the bag using a spray nozzle. (Note: Massaging the bag needs to be done very gently as the seeds and young sprouts are very fragile.)

17. Place the sprout bag back into the plastic bag and hang.

18. After the seeds have sprouted according to the sprouting time indicated in the sprouting instructions chart, expose them to indirect sunlight for a day or two until small green leaves appear. (Some sprouts do not require this step. These sprouts will be noted in the sprouting instructions chart.) Do not expose the sprouts to direct sunlight, as it is too harsh for them.

19. After the seeds are fully sprouted and the leaves appear, place the sprouts in a bowl of cool water and swirl them around with a clean hand. This will remove hulls that will float to the top of the water. Scoop the hulls out with your hand or with a spoon.

20. Drain the sprouts.

21. Allow the sprouts to dry for at least eight hours before you refrigerate them.

22. Store the sprouts in the refrigerator for up to ten days, though they are best if eaten as soon as possible.

The Tray/Basket Method

The proponents of the tray method will tell you that the advantage to sprouting in trays is it allows the sprouts to grow vertically as they were meant to grow. In fact, this method is also called **vertical sprouting**. Another advantage is that it can provide a higher yield of sprouts as it provides a large surface area, exposing more sprouts to air and sun.

The primary disadvantage to this method is that the equipment needed to employ it is a little more cumbersome than the jar or bag. The method also takes up more space.

Necessities

- Jar
- Tray or basket for sprouting (*see description in Chapter 2*)
- Measuring spoons
- Sieve
- Organic sprouting seeds (*The suggested amount of seeds are indicated on the chart shown later in this chapter*)
- Water (If you live in a place with clean and reliable drinking tap water, using it is perfectly fine. If you should not drink your tap water, use bottled drinking water.)
- Plastic cover or tent (large enough to accommodate your sprout tray or basket)

Procedure

1. Examine seeds to be sprouted, discarding any discolored seeds, hulls, broken seeds, or any foreign matter.
2. Place the seeds in a small bowl and cover them with water.
3. Allow the seeds to sit in the water for ten minutes.
4. Pour the seeds and water from the bowl into a sieve.
5. Run cool water over the seeds in the sieve to clean them.
6. Place seeds in wide-mouth jar.

7. Cover the top of the jar with plastic strainer top. (You can also use cheesecloth or any top that will allow the sprouting seeds to breathe and be used as a strainer.)

8. Add cool water to jar. (A good rule of thumb is that you add four times the amount of water as the amount of seeds.)

9. Soak the seeds according to the soaking time indicated in the sprouting instructions chart.

10. Pour the water off through the strainer top, leaving the seeds in the jar. As you pour the water off, swirl the seeds around in the jar.

11. Spread the soaked seeds/sprouts evenly in the tray.

12. Place a clear cover (plastic bag or plastic cover) that has some ventilation holes in it over the tray.

13. The tray/basket can be placed in a well-lit place, though not in direct sunlight.

14. Place the tray so that there can be ventilation on the bottom. How you do this will be determined by what kind of tray or basket you use. The point is to allow ventilation from the top and bottom.

15. Rinse and drain the sprouts three times a day for the recommended sprouting time indicated in the sprouting instructions chart. This can be accomplished in several ways. You can heavily mist or spray your sprouts over a sink. If you choose this method, be sure to spray the sides of the tray, as well as the sprouts, to clean the sides of the tray and allow water to run under the sprouts along the length and width of the tray. Also, hardy sprouts such as alfalfa can stand direct spray rinsing, while the more delicate green and leafy sprouts such as radish and mustard should be rinsed indirectly. To indirectly rinse in a tray, spray the sides of the tray and allow the water that runs off the sides of the tray to wash over the sprouts. Another way to rinse sprouts in a tray is to immerse the entire tray in a bath, slosh it around a bit, and then remove the tray, allowing the water to drain out the bottom.

16. Allow the tray to drain a bit over the sink.

17. Replace the plastic cover.

18. Place the tray back in a well-lit place, though not in direct sunlight.

19. After the seeds are fully sprouted and the leaves appear, place the sprouts in a bowl of cool water and swirl them around with a clean hand. This will remove hulls that will float to the top of the water. Scoop the hulls out with your hand or with a spoon.

20. Drain the sprouts.

21. Allow the sprouts to dry for at least eight hours before you refrigerate them.

22. Store the sprouts in the refrigerator for up to ten days, though they are best eaten as soon as possible.

The Soil Method

The soil method has the same advantages and disadvantages as the tray method with one great distinction: The nutritional value of sprouts germinated in water is quite high, but when you add soil to the mix, the value is even greater. Also, germinating and growing in soil will allow you to advance the greenness of your garden as you can grow grasses such as wheat and greens such as sunflower.

The basic steps of the soil method are described below. Chapter 5 will go into much more detail about this advanced method of sprouting and growing.

Necessities

- Jar
- Tray or basket for sprouting (*see description in Chapter 2*)
- Opaque top for tray
- Soil (*see soil description in Chapter 2*)
- Measuring spoons
- Sieve

- Organic sprouting seeds (*The suggested amount of seeds are indicated on the chart shown later in this chapter*)
- Water (If you live in a place with clean and reliable drinking tap water, using it is perfectly fine. If you should not drink your tap water, use bottled drinking water.)

Procedure

1. Examine seeds to be sprouted, discarding any discolored seeds, hulls, broken seeds, or any foreign matter.
2. Place the seeds in a small bowl and cover them with water.
3. Allow the seeds to sit in the water for ten minutes.
4. Pour the seeds and water from the bowl into a sieve.
5. Run cool water over the seeds in the sieve to clean them.
6. Place seeds in wide-mouth jar.
7. Cover the top of the jar with plastic strainer top. (You can also use cheesecloth or any top that will allow the sprouting seeds to breathe and be used as a strainer.)
8. Add cool water to jar. (A good rule of thumb is that you add four times the amount of water as the amount of seeds.)
9. Soak the seeds according to the soaking time indicated in the sprouting instructions chart.
10. Pour the water off through the strainer top, leaving the seeds in the jar. As you pour the water off, swirl the seeds around in the jar.
11. Spread ¼ to ½ inch of moist soil evenly over the bottom of the tray.
12. If the soil is not saturated, saturate it prior to adding the seeds. To saturate the soil, give it water until it is thoroughly soaked and cannot take any more water without forming puddles. The combination of the water and soil provides the seeds with a nutritious medium that kick-starts their germination process.

13. Spread the soaked seeds/sprouts evenly in the tray. Because you will be covering the tray, covering the seeds is not necessary. Covering the seeds with soil allows soil to cling to the seeds and you end up with dirty sprouts.

14. Place an opaque cover over the tray of soil and seeds.

15. The tray/basket can be set aside for a couple of days. You can keep the tray anywhere out of the way and out of direct sunlight.

16. After two days, take a look at your sprouts. In some case, the sprouts may be lifting the lid to look at you.

17. Place the tray back in direct sunlight for two days.

18. Water the sprouts twice a day during this period.

19. There are several ways you can harvest your grown sprouts. One way is to snip off the tops with a pair of scissors. To do this, make sure that your greens are dry and do not water them the day you harvest them. Instead, prior to harvesting, use your hand to brush the soil and hulls off of greens. You might brush them the same way you would pet a dog or cat with the palm of your hand. This will clear away any soil or hulls that remain on the leaves. After brushing, snip the tops off just above the soil. An alternative method of harvesting is just to pull the entire sprout out of the dirt and rinse it off in a colander. The advantage to the cutting method is that there will probably be a number of late sprouters. By snipping the greens that have grown, you will not disturb those sprouters that like to sleep in. If you have cut your greens, return the tray to the sunlight and wait for your second harvest.

20. If you pulled your greens, rinse and drain them.

21. Allow the sprouts to dry for at least eight hours before you refrigerate them.

22. Store the sprouts in the refrigerator for up to ten days, though they are best eaten as soon as possible.

Exceptions

As you proceed through this chapter and you read through the table below detailing the preferred methods of sprouting, soak times, germination times, and more, you will come a across a seed type that does not require soaking. Arugula is one of a family of seeds that are known as **mucilaginous**. Mucilaginous seeds are those that produce a moist and sticky gel when they get wet. Other seeds you may wish to sprout that do not appear on this list that are mucilaginous are basil, cress, and flax. When these seeds come in contact with water, they produce a gel sac that surrounds the seed. As a result, soaking them turns them into a sticky mess.

The directions for sprouting are only general guidelines. It is suggested that as you proceed, you do your homework carefully with each type of seed you plan to sprout. *The chart later in this chapter will give you more details as to how to germinate each of the specific seeds.* You may also wish to expand your research beyond this book. Further research can educate you on subjects such as ways to expand your sprouting operations through automated sprouting systems and constructing larger grow houses. There is an Appendix at the end of this book that will point you in the right direction for continuing your sprout education.

Whether you choose to sprout using a jar, tube, tray, bag, or soil, you will find that once you get things up and running, sprouting seeds is a simple process. If you enjoy the process and the fresh produce it offers you, chances are that you will branch out and employ several, if not all, of the sprouting methods. You may find that the method(s) you employ will be determined by the season. Sprout growers in Florida will operate on a much different sprouting calendar than sprout growers in Montana. Apartment dwellers in New York may find that they have to grow differently than homeowners with large yards and lots of space in Nebraska. That being said, growing sprouts is an equal opportunity activity that anyone can participate in.

The following table spells out some of the specifics of sprouting the seeds described in the previous chapter. The table describes the preferred methods of sprouting the specific seeds, good amounts to sprout with the equipment described in Chapter 2, recommended soaking times, and approximate times to germination. The table also contains special instructions that may be necessary to germinate each of the indicated seeds.

As you become more experienced in growing sprouts, you will probably find that you will develop your own methods, as well as your own soaking and germination times. As stated earlier, it is a good idea to taste your sprouts with each rinsing to help you determine when your sprouts are ready to use as per your tastes. The times indicated on the table are only suggestions.

As you grow, make notes as to what works and what does not work. Note what sprouts you enjoy and which sprouts you dislike. Note the sprouts that grow well using a jar and those that do better in a bag, a tray, or in soil.

The table's special instructions will only touch briefly on the soil method as described above. *Chapter 5 will spend a little more time and get a little more specific about the soil method and the various ways to grow a variety of seeds in soil.*

Sprout Variety	Planting Method(s)	Amount of Seed Needed	Soaking Time	Sprouting Time	Special Instructions
Adzuki-bean	Jar, tube, or bag	½ cup	12 hours	2 to 5 days	These beans will change color and become paler as they soak. If you notice that some of the beans remain dark after 12 hours, allow them to soak a little longer.

Sprout Variety	Planting Method(s)	Amount of Seed Needed	Soaking Time	Sprouting Time	Special Instructions
Alfafa	Jar, tube, bag, tray or soil	3 Tbsp.	3 to 6 hours	4 to 6 days	Allow to green in indirect sunlight on final day.
Almond	Jar, tube, or bag	2 to 3 cups	8 to 12 hours	1 to 2 days	Allow to green in indirect sunlight on final day.
Amaranth	Jar, tube, bag, or tray	1 cup	3 to 5 hours	2 to 3 days	Rinse frequently every four to six hours.
Arugula	Bag or soil	3 Tbsp.	No soaking required	5 to 6 days	Try growing these sprouts between several damp pieces of white paper towels.
Barley (unhulled)	Jar, tube, or bag	1 cup	6 to 8 hours	6 to 9 days	This is barley for grass. Hulled barley will not sprout for this purpose.
Black turtle bean	Jar, tube, or bag	½ to 1 cup	8 to 12 hours	2 to 4 days	Grow only until sprout tail is ¼ inch long. These sprouts need to be cooked before they are eaten.
Broccoli	Jar, tube, bag, tray, or soil	2 to 3 Tbsp.	6 to 12 hours	3 to 4 days	As you begin to soak, be sure to push down any floating seeds as these seeds tend to be floaters.
Buckwheat (hulled)	Jar, tube, or bag	1 cup	15 to 20 minutes	1 to 2 days	Treat unhulled buckwheat as you would barley.

Sprout Variety	Planting Method(s)	Amount of Seed Needed	Soaking Time	Sprouting Time	Special Instructions
Cabbage	Jar, tube, or bag	2 to 3 Tbsp.	6 hours	4 to 5 days	Shake these seeds well as you rinse them because they are so small.
Chickpea (also called garbanzo)	Jar, tube, or bag	1 cup	12 hours	2 to 4 days	These beans are easier to digest if you allow them to soak for the full 12 hours.
Chive	Jar, tube, bag, or tray	2 to 3 Tbsp.	8 hours	10 to 14 days	As you begin to soak, be sure to push down any floating seeds as these seeds tend to be floaters.
Clover	Jar, tube, bag, or tray	2 to 3 Tbsp.	4 to 6 hours	4 to 6 days	Clover sprouts best in a tray. It grows quickly and you will have a huge yield.
Fenugreek	Jar, tube, bag, or tray	4 Tbsp.	6 to 8 hours	2 to 5 days	Do not let this sprout grow beyond 1 inch in length.
Green Pea	Jar, tube, or bag	1 cup	8 to 12 hours	2 to 3 days	Afer soaking, discard any hard peas. They are easy to spot as they do not swell with water.
Lentil	Jar, tube, or bag	¾ cup	8 hours	2 to 4 days	Be sure to rinse these at least three times a day.
Lettuce	Jar, tube, bag, or soil	3 Tbsp.	No soaking required	4 to 5 days	Soil is best for lettuce. See instruction in Chapter 5.

Sprout Variety	Planting Method(s)	Amount of Seed Needed	Soaking Time	Sprouting Time	Special Instructions
Millet	Jar, tube, or bag	1 to 2 cups	6 to 8 hours	1 to 2 days	This is very easy to sprout and best sprouts in a jar.
Mung bean	Jar, tube, or bag	½ cup	6 to 12 hours	2 to 5 days	After soaking, discard any hard beans. They are easy to spot as they do not swell with water.
Mustard Seed	Jar, tube, bag, tray, or soil	3 Tbsp.	6 hours	3 to 5 days	As you begin to soak, be sure to push down any floating seeds, as these seeds to be floaters. Also, place in indirect sun on day five.
Oats	Jar, tube, bag, or soil	1 to 2 cups	6 to 8 hours	1 to 3 days	Oats are difficult to sprout, but very good soaked. Give them the one to three days of sprouting time.
Onion	Jar, tube, bag, tray, or soil	1 to 2 Tbsp.	6 to 12 hours	4 to 5 days	As you begin to soak, be sure to push down any floating seeds, as these seeds tend o be floaters.
Peanuts	Jar, tube, or bag	1 cup	6 to 12 hours	2 to 4 days	Do not forget to taste with each rinse. Peanuts are especially good with a shorter sprout time.

Sprout Variety	Planting Method(s)	Amount of Seed Needed	Soaking Time	Sprouting Time	Special Instructions
Pumpkin	Jar, tube, or bag	1 cup	6 hours	1 to 2 days	Another seed that is best only soaked, as they are difficult to sprout.
Quinoa	Jar, tube, or bag	1 cup	2 to 4 hours	2 to 4 days	Rinse these seeds six to eight times before you soak them. The extra rinses improve the taste.
Radish	Jar, tube, bag, tray, or soil	3 Tbsp.	6 to 8 hours	3 to 5 days	Best sprouted in bags as they do vey well with imrpoved air circulation.
Rye	Jar, tube, bag, tray, or soil	1 cup	6 to 12 hours	2 to 3 days	Make sure these sprout in a cool (70°) environment.
Sesame	Jar, tbe, or bag	1 to 2 cups	6 to 8 hours	1 to 3 days	Rinse four times a day.
Soybean	Jar, tube, or bag	¾ cup	8 to 12 hours	2 to 6 days	If you decide to try sprouting soybeans, start with a small amount because they have a taste that many find disagreeable.
Sunflower	Jar, tube, bag, or soil	1 cup	1 to 4 hours	1 to 2 days	Taste frequently during soaking as these are easy to over-soak.
Wheat	Jar, tube, bag, tray, or soil	1 cup	8 to 12 hours	2 to 3 days	These grow quickly so remember to taste with each rinse.

As you begin to learn the ways of sprouting, start with the jar or the bag as these are the simplest and most straightforward methods of sprouting seeds. You will note that all of the seeds listed above, with the exception of arugula, can be sprouted in a jar or bag. All those seeds noted as being jar and bag sproutable are exceedingly simple to sprout using either of those methods.

Note that there are several seeds listed above (almonds and pumpkin seeds, for example) that are only soaked rather than fully sprouted. The reason for this is that the seeds are ready in a shorter period of time and all that these seeds need to be edible is a short soak. Nuts like almonds will not develop a sprout but will only bulge. If these seeds are soaked too long, they will rot.

You have a handful of seeds that are itching to get out of their shells. Jump in and get started.

CASE STUDY: JIM MUMM

Jim Mumm
MUMM'S SPROUTING SEEDS LTD. Certified organic seeds for sprouting
mumms@sprouting.com
www.sprouting.com

The Mumm family has been growing their own sprouts since the early 1970s. The company went "back to the land" in the mid-1970s, and alfalfa seed was one of the crops on the small farm the Mumms own. In about 1982, Mumm's made its first sprout sale to a Vancouver health food wholesaler. Since then, the business of growing and supplying certified organic sprouting seeds has grown so much that their farm has become their side project. Mumm's Sprouting Seeds has been a certified organic sprouting seed supplier since 1982.

Jim Mumm says he grows sprouts because they are good food and fresh produce year-round. "We have our favorites: red clover, sunflower, radish, garlic chives, fennel, and some blends that contain broccoli, which we grow at home," he said. "We usually have lots of sprouts to choose from in the fridge at work because we are always testing some of the

60 varieties that we sell."

Mumm said, "The greatest health benefit to growing and consuming sprouts is that sprouts are the original health food, a great source of chlorophyll and antioxidants."

Mumm believes that the best method for home sprouting depends on the seed type and the amount of sprouts needed. "There's nothing wrong with the old 'jar and screen' method for most smaller seeds and short sprouts.Tray-type sprouters produce attractive results and are great for taller shoots. Sprouting bags are good for larger seeds and short sprouts. They're also good for mung beans. Automatic sprouters are good for those growing large quantities of sprouts."

He said that there are certain types of seeds that are easier to grow than others. "The easiest types are mixes of peas/beans or lentils. They are ready in three days and very forgiving," Mumm said. "The hardest are the mucilaginous seeds — arugula, basil, chia, cress, flax. They do not like to be soaked in water, and do best with just misting or spritzing once or twice a day. Some seeds like beet and coriander have hard-to-remove hulls. They are best sprouted in soil. Chemically treated seeds, of course, shouldn't be sprouted."

"Non-organic seeds may have been treated with chemicals, even with chemicals that aren't approved for use on food crops, sometimes with as much as eight applications of herbicides and/or pesticides per growing season. Certified organic seeds are your guarantee that you are pur-chasing seeds that are the best possible for your health and the health of the soil, air, and water tables, with the added benefit of knowing that you are supporting small-scale, sustainable organic farmers.

Jim Mumm shares his knowledge and experience with those new to sprouting by advising, "Just do it! It's easy and you can learn while you grow. Sprouts are easy to grow. Just soak the seeds and rinse twice a day."

Here are Jim Mumm's tips on growing sunflower shoots:

1. Use a tray to grow sunflower sprouts.
2. Soak one layer of seed in the bottom of a sprouting tray for two to six hours.

3. Rinse or spritz twice a day.
4. At about day three when roots start to come though the bottom of the tray, put the tray in a Pyrex dish with ¼ inch of water in the bottom.
5. Rinse or spritz twice a day and change the water the roots are in once a day.
6. When the leaves start to form, cover them with a clear plastic bag to retain condensation. This will help them shed their hulls.
7. From day ten to 12, remove from tray and cut roots off.

Mumm's favorite dressing to use contains:

- Juice from ½ to 1 lemon
- A little less olive oil than lemon juice
- Minced garlic (to taste)
- Oregano (to taste)
- Basil, dried and crushed (to taste)
- Ground pepper to taste
- Touch of salt

Try this dressing on a twist on a traditional Greek salad: Instead of using lettuce in your salad, use sunflower shoots.

Chapter 5

How to Grow

> *"Don't go through life, grow through life."*
> — Eric Butterworth, minister

After you have mastered the art of sprouting, you may consider taking the next step with your sprouts and trying your hand at growing. The difference between sprouting and growing is the addition of soil. Essentially, you will be starting an indoor garden. To those of you who have a house or apartment full of plants, this may not seem like a big step. Here, though, we examine methods of growing edible plants.

There are some advantages and disadvantages to employing the soil method of sprouting and growing. The biggest disadvantage is that it is somewhat cumbersome as compared to the simplicity of a jar. You can sprout and green alfalfa in a jar in a shorter period of time, for less cost, and in a much less messy environment than you can in soil. The advantages to using soil, however, are that the produce will have a higher nutritional value and, if arranged properly, can be a very pretty addition to your living space.

As you go over the chart in Chapter 4 that details how to sprout a variety of seeds, there are a number of seeds that suggest soil as a method of growth.

This chapter will detail the strategies behind using soil to sprout and/or grow each of these seeds.

You can begin exploring the soil method by reviewing the basic steps laid out in Chapter 4. If you were to simply follow these steps with any of the seeds that the soil method is suggested for, you would probably have some amount of success because the method is quite simple.

The goal of this chapter is to spell out some slight variations in the soil method that, with practice and patience, will increase your chances of success. The description of soil method specifics will start with the simple and progress to the slightly complex. Note that here, slightly complex is still fairly simple.

Alfafa

Necessities

- Jar
- Tray (*see tray description in Chapter 2*)
- Opaque top for tray
- Soil (*see soil description in Chapter 2*)
- Measuring spoons
- Sieve
- 3 Tbsp. of organic alfalfa seeds
- Colander
- Water (If you live in a place with clean and reliable drinking tap water, using it is perfectly fine. If you should not drink your tap water, use bottled drinking water.)

Procedure

1. Examine seeds to be sprouted, discarding any discolored seeds, hulls, broken seeds, or any foreign matter.
2. Place the seeds in a small bowl and cover them with water.

3. Allow the seeds to sit in the water for ten minutes.

4. Pour the seeds and water from the bowl into a sieve.

5. Run cool water over the seeds in the sieve to clean them.

6. Place seeds in wide-mouth jar.

7. Cover the top of the jar with plastic strainer top. (You can also use cheesecloth or any top that will allow the sprouting seeds to breathe and be used as a strainer.)

8. Add cool water to jar. (A good rule of thumb is that you add four times the amount of water as the amount of seeds.)

9. Soak the seeds for three to six hours.

10. Pour the water off through the strainer top, leaving the seeds in the jar. As you pour the water off, swirl the seeds around in the jar.

11. Spread ¼ to ½ inch of moist soil evenly over the bottom of the tray.

12. If the soil is not saturated, saturate it prior to adding the seeds.

13. Spread the soaked seeds/sprouts evenly in the tray. It is not necessary to cover the seeds with soil.

14. Place an opaque cover over the tray of soil and seeds.

15. Set the tray in an out-of-the-way location at room temperature for two days.

16. After two days, look at your sprouts to check for moisture and little sprouts popping up above soil.

17. Place the tray back in a well-lit place in indirect sunlight for two days.

18. Water the sprouts twice a day during this period. The best method of watering these little sprouts is to use a spray bottle that provides a fine mist.

19. Harvest the alfalfa by pulling the entire sprout out of the dirt.

20. Rinse the sprouts off in a colander.

21. Allow the sprouts to dry in a cool place (room temperature) for at least eight hours before you refrigerate them.

22. Store the sprouts in the refrigerator for up to ten days, though they are best eaten as soon as possible.

Arugula, Lettuce, or Mustard

Necessities

- Tray (*see tray description in Chapter 2*)
- Opaque top for tray
- Soil (*see soil description in Chapter 2*)
- Measuring spoons
- Colander
- 3 Tbsp. of organic arugula, lettuce, or mustard seeds
- Water (If you live in a place with clean and reliable drinking tap water, using it is perfectly fine. If you cannot drink your tap water, use bottled drinking water.)

Procedure

1. Examine seeds to be sprouted, discarding any discolored seeds, hulls, broken seeds, or any foreign matter.
2. Place the seeds in a small bowl and cover them with water.
3. Allow the seeds to sit in the water for ten minutes.
4. Pour the seeds and water from the bowl into a sieve.
5. Run cool water over the seeds in the sieve to clean them.
6. Spread ¼ to ½ inch of moist soil evenly over the bottom of the tray.
7. If the soil is not saturated, do so prior to adding the seeds.
8. Spread the seeds evenly in the tray. It is not necessary to cover the seeds with soil.
9. Place an opaque cover over the tray of soil and seeds.
10. Set the tray in an out-of-the-way location at room temperature for two to three days.

11. Check the moisture of the soil after about a day and a half. The soil should be moist. If it is not, spray it with a fine mist.

12. After two days, take a look at your sprouts. If they have begun to cast off their hulls, they are ready to see some light. If they have not yet begun to shed hulls, give them another day of darkness.

13. Place the tray back in a well-lit place in indirect sunlight for two days.

14. Water the sprouts twice a day during this period. The best method of watering these little sprouts is to use a spray bottle that provides a fine mist.

15. Harvest the arugula, lettuce, or mustard by pulling the entire sprout out of the dirt.

16. Gently rinse the sprouts off in a colander.

17. Allow the sprouts to dry for at least eight hours before you refrigerate them.

18. Store the sprouts in the refrigerator for up to ten days, though they are best eaten as soon as possible.

Broccoli and Radish

Necessities

- Jar
- Tray (*see tray description in Chapter 2*)
- Opaque top for tray
- Soil (*see soil description in Chapter 2*)
- Measuring spoons
- Sieve
- 2 to 3 Tbsp. of organic broccoli or radish seeds
- Water (If you live in a place with clean and reliable drinking tap water, using it is perfectly fine. If you should not drink your tap water, use bottled drinking water.)

Procedure

1. Examine seeds to be sprouted, discarding any discolored seeds, hulls, broken seeds, or any foreign matter.

2. Place the seeds in a small bowl and cover them with water.

3. Allow the seeds to sit in the water for ten minutes.

4. Pour the seeds and water from the bowl into a sieve.

5. Run cool water over the seeds in the sieve to clean them.

6. Place seeds in wide-mouth jar.

7. Cover the top of the jar with plastic strainer top. (You can also use cheesecloth or any top that will allow the sprouting seeds to breathe and be used as a strainer.)

8. Add cool water to jar. (A good rule of thumb is that you add four times the amount of water as the amount of seeds.)

9. Soak the seeds for eight to 12 hours. Make sure that the seeds produce a very small root before you proceed to the next step. Seeing the root tells you that the seeds are viable and alive.

10. Pour the water off through the strainer top, leaving the seeds in the jar. As you pour the water off, swirl the seeds around in the jar.

11. Spread ¼ to ½ inch of moist soil evenly over the bottom of the tray.

12. If the soil is not saturated, do so prior to adding the seeds.

13. Spread the soaked seeds/sprouts very thinly and evenly in the tray. It is not necessary to cover the seeds with soil.

14. Place an opaque cover over the tray of soil and seeds.

15. Set the tray in an out-of-the-way location at room temperature for two days.

16. After one day, take a look at your sprouts.

17. If the soil is not still saturated, saturate it using a very fine, gentle mist.

18. Return the sprouts to darkness for another day.

19. On the third day, place the tray in a well-lit place in indirect sunlight

for two days.

20. Water the sprouts twice a day during this period. The best method of watering these little sprouts is to do so indirectly. To do this, water very gently from one side of the tray as you tilt the tray slightly to allow the water to run down the length of the tray.

21. Do not water for eight hours prior to harvesting, as you want to harvest dry greens.

22. Before you harvest, gently brush off the tops of the greens to rid them of any soil or loose hulls.

23. Harvest the broccoli (or radish) by snipping the plant at the level of the dirt.

24. Store the sprouts in the refrigerator for up to seven days, though they are best eaten as soon as possible.

Chives (Garlic) and Onion

Necessities

- Jar
- Tray (*see tray description in Chapter 2*)
- Opaque top for tray
- Soil (*see soil description in Chapter 2*)
- Measuring spoons
- Sieve
- 2 to 3 Tbsp. of organic chive or onion seeds
- Water (If you live in a place with clean and reliable drinking tap water, using it is perfectly fine. If you should not drink your tap water, use bottled drinking water.)

Procedure

1. Examine seeds to be sprouted, discarding any discolored seeds, hulls, broken seeds, or any foreign matter.

2. Place the seeds in a small bowl and cover them with water.

3. Allow the seeds to sit in the water for ten minutes.

4. Pour the seeds and water from the bowl into a sieve.

5. Run cool water over the seeds in the sieve to clean them.

6. Place seeds in wide-mouth jar.

7. Cover the top of the jar with plastic strainer top. (You can also use cheesecloth or any top that will allow the sprouting seeds to breathe and be used as a strainer.)

8. Add cool water to jar. (A good rule of thumb is that you add four times the amount of water as the amount of seeds.)

9. Soak the seeds for eight to 12 hours. Make sure that the seeds produce a very small root before you proceed to the next step.

10. Pour the water off through the strainer top, leaving the seeds in the jar. As you pour the water off, swirl the seeds around in the jar.

11. Spread ¼ to ½ inch of moist soil evenly over the bottom of the tray.

12. If the soil is not saturated, do so prior to adding the seeds.

13. Spread the soaked seeds/sprouts very thinly and evenly in the tray. It is not necessary to cover the seeds with soil.

14. Place an opaque cover over the tray of soil and seeds.

15. Set the tray in an out-of-the-way location at room temperature for three to four days.

16. After one day, take a look at your sprouts.

17. If the soil is not still saturated, saturate the soil using a very fine, gentle mist.

18. Return the sprouts to darkness. Onions and chives can take a very long time to sprout, so do not give up on them. They may take as long as seven days.

19. Keep the soil saturated by misting it on a daily basis.

20. Once you see green, move your sprouts to a place with indirect sunlight.

21. Water the sprouts twice a day during this period. The best method of watering these little sprouts is to gently mist the sprouts and soil.

22. You can harvest the sprouts at any point after they green, but they are best at about 1 inch in length.

23. Harvest the onions or chives by pulling the entire sprout out of the dirt.

24. Rinse the sprouts off in a colander.

25. Allow the sprouts to dry in a cool place for at least eight hours before you refrigerate them.

26. Store the sprouts in the refrigerator for up to two weeks, though they are best eaten as soon as possible.

Oat, Rye, or Wheat

Growing these grains in soil provides a grass (oat grass, rye grass, or wheatgrass). These grasses are not eaten (except by pets such as cats and dogs) but rather consumed as juice. *Recipes for using wheatgrass, rye grass, and oat grass will be given in Chapter 13. You will also learn how you can add these grasses to your pet's diet in Chapter 15.*

Necessities

- Jar (needs to be capable of holding at least 4 cups)
- Tray (*see tray description in Chapter 2*)
- Opaque top for tray
- Soil (*see soil description in Chapter 2*)
- Measuring cup
- Sieve
- 1 cup of organic oats, rye, or wheat
- Colander
- Water (If you live in a place with clean and reliable drinking tap water, using it is perfectly fine. If you should not drink your tap water, use bottled drinking water.)

Procedure

1. Examine grains to be sprouted, discarding any discolored seeds, hulls, broken seeds, or any foreign matter.
2. Place the grains in a bowl and cover with water.
3. Allow the grains to sit in the water for ten minutes.
4. Pour the grains and water from the bowl into a sieve.
5. Run cool water over the grains in the sieve to clean them.
6. Place grains in wide-mouth jar.
7. Cover the top of the jar with plastic strainer top. (You can also use cheesecloth or any top that will allow the sprouting grain to breathe and be used as a strainer.)
8. Add 3 cups of cool water to jar.
9. Soak the grains for eight to 12 hours.
10. Pour the water off through the strainer top, leaving the grains in the jar. As you pour the water off, swirl the grains around in the jar.
11. Allow the jar to rest in a cool, dark place at a 45-degree angle with the top facing down to allow the excess water to drain off. Make sure that the grains do not completely cover the opening in the strainer.
12. Rinse and drain the sprouts three times a day for three days.
13. Each time you rinse and drain the grains, swirl the water in the jar to move the sprouting seeds around.
14. After you rinse and drain, allow the jar to rest in a cool, dark place at a 45-degree angle with the top facing down to allow the excess water to drain off. Make sure that the grains do not completely cover the opening in the strainer.
15. Spread ½ to 1 inch of moist soil evenly over the bottom of the tray.
16. If the soil is not saturated, saturate it prior to adding the grains.
17. Spread the soaked grain sprouts evenly in the tray. It is not necessary to cover the seeds with soil.
18. Place an opaque cover over the tray of soil and seeds.

19. The tray can be set in an out-of-the-way location at room temperature for three or four days.
20. Keep your grass watered during this period by lightly misting your lawn.
21. When the grass is a couple inches tall, it will begin to push the top tray up.
22. When you see that the tray is being pushed up, remove the cover.
23. Place the tray back in a well-lit place, in direct sunlight for as long as ten days.
24. Water the grass daily during this period. The best method of watering these little sprouts is to use a spray bottle that provides a fine mist.
25. Harvest the grass by cutting with a pair of scissors just above the soil line. After you harvest the grass, there is no need to rinse.
26. Store the grass in a glass container in the refrigerator for up to one week, though it is best consumed as soon as possible.
27. Like a lawn, your grass will continue to grow after you cut it. These crops are good for two or three clippings before you will want to start anew. You will find that the grass will get tougher on each re-growth.

Sunflower

If you have never grown or eaten sunflower sprouts or greens, you are missing one of the greatest culinary delights that is easily available to you. Whether you eat them fresh or mix them into bread dough, you will return again and again to their tender and mildly nutty taste. It is very easy to sit down and munch them like popcorn, though you will be getting much more nutritional value from those sunflower greens than you might get from popcorn.

Necessities

- Jar (needs to be capable of holding at least 4 cups)
- Tray (*see tray description in Chapter 2*)
- Opaque top for tray
- Soil (*see soil description in Chapter 2*)
- Measuring cup
- Sieve
- 1 to 2 cups of organic sunflower seeds
- Colander
- Water (If you live in a place with clean and reliable drinking tap water, using it is perfectly fine. If you should not drink your tap water, use bottled drinking water.)

Procedure

1. Examine sunflower seeds to be sprouted, discarding any discolored seeds, hulls, broken seeds, or any foreign matter.
2. Place the sunflower seeds in a bowl and cover with water.
3. Allow the sunflower seeds to sit in the water for ten minutes.
4. Pour the sunflower seeds and water from the bowl into a sieve.
5. Run cool water over the sunflower seeds in the sieve to clean them.
6. Place sunflower seeds in wide-mouth jar.
7. Cover the top of the jar with plastic strainer top. (You can also use cheesecloth or any top that will allow the sprouting grain to breathe and be used as a strainer.)
8. Add 3 to 4 cups of cool water to jar.
9. Soak the sunflower seeds for eight to 12 hours.
10. Pour the water off through the strainer top, leaving the sunflower seeds in the jar. As you pour the water off, swirl the sunflower seeds around in the jar.
11. Allow the jar to rest in a cool, dark place at a 45-degree angle with the top facing down to allow the excess water to drain off. Make sure

that the sunflower seeds do not completely cover the opening in the strainer.

12. Rinse and drain the sprouts three times a day for two days.

13. By the second day, you should begin to see tiny roots beginning to break through the seed shells.

14. When you notice the roots breaking through, give the sprouts one last rinse and swirl.

15. Spread ½ to 1 inch of moist soil evenly over the bottom of the tray.

16. If the soil is not saturated, saturate it prior to adding the grain.

17. Spread the soaked sunflower seed sprouts evenly in the tray. It is not necessary to cover the seeds with soil.

18. Make sure that the sunflower seeds are evenly distributed and in contact with the soil. Make sure that the sunflower seeds are not piled on top of each other.

19. Place an opaque cover over the tray of soil and seeds.

20. Set the tray in an out-of-the-way location at room temperature for two or three days.

21. Keep your greens watered during this period by lightly misting your little sprouts.

22. When the greens are a couple inches tall, they will begin to push the top tray up. After they push the top of the tray up, remove the cover.

23. Place the tray back in a well-lit place in direct sunlight for two or three days.

24. Water the greens daily during this period. The best method of watering these little sprouts is to use a spray bottle that provides a fine mist.

25. Harvest the greens by cutting them with a pair of scissor just above the soil line. After this, there is no need to rinse.

26. After you clip your first harvest, you can place the tray back in the sunlight and continue to mist for a day or two. Additional greens will

> appear and you can reap another harvest. The second harvest will not be as bountiful as the first, but it will be just as tasty.
>
> 27. Store the sunflower greens in a glass container in the refrigerator for up to two weeks, though it is best consumed as soon as possible.

A question that might arise as you harvest each of the crops above is: Can I just plow what is left in the tray under and use the dirt again? Do not reuse the soil for subsequent growings. The best use for the soil that remains after you harvest your sprouts is the compost bin. It is not advisable to reuse the soil because nutrients have been removed from it by your crop. Composting the soil will return the nutrients. You can find great directions on how to establish an indoor compost bin, complete with earthworms, at the website of the Organic Consumers Association (**www.organicconsumers. org/organic/compost.cfm**).

If you are serious about establishing indoor growing, composting will offer you a source of nutrient-rich humus to add to whatever soil you use to grow. **Humus** is partially decomposed organic matter that is the source of nutrients for plant life. Humus is a great addition to the soil you use for growing sprouts.

Soil-Free Growing

You can grow several of the crops listed above without soil. The grasses and sunflower greens can be grown indoors in much the same manner as the soil method, but without the soil. You may find this to be an interesting experiment because you will discover what soil does for the taste of these items. Some people will swear by the soil-free method of growing and the resulting taste, while others will swear that soil-free sprouting tastes like cardboard and soil makes all the difference. However, the difference in taste is very difficult to account for, so you will need to be the judge. Follow these simple instructions to grow wheatgrass and sunflower greens soil-free and compare them to what you will grow in soil.

Necessities

- Jar
- Basket (This basket needs to be a large bamboo basket with a wide weave. The bamboo should be natural, with no paint or coating of any kind)
- Greenhouse tent (The requirement here is that you enclose your garden completely in a clear bubble. Simple plastic wrap can work for this, but it is better to construct a larger area that will provide more circulation. This is easily accomplished with several coat hangers and heavy-duty plastic wrap. Your goal is simply to surround your basket of sprouts in a clear bubble; it is not necessary that the tent be air-tight.)
- Measuring cup
- Sieve
- ½ cup of organic sunflower seeds, oat, rye, or wheat
- Colander
- Water (If you live in a place with clean and reliable drinking tap water, using it is perfectly fine. If you should not drink your tap water, use bottled drinking water.)

Procedure

1. Examine sunflower seeds or grains to be sprouted, discarding any discolored seeds, hulls, broken seeds, or any foreign matter.
2. Place the sunflower seeds or grains in a bowl and cover with water.
3. Allow the sunflower seeds to sit in the water for ten minutes.
4. Pour the sunflower seeds and water from the bowl into a sieve and run cool water over the seeds to clean them.
5. Place sunflower seeds in wide-mouth jar.
6. Cover the top of the jar with plastic strainer top. (You can also use

cheesecloth or any top that will allow the sprouting grain to breathe and be used as a strainer.)

7. Add 2 to 3 cups of cool water to jar.

8. Soak the sunflower seeds or grains for eight to 12 hours.

9. Pour the water off through the strainer top, leaving the sunflower seeds in the jar. As you pour the water off, swirl the sunflower seeds around in the jar.

10. Rinse and drain the sprouts.

11. Fill the jar of sunflower seeds or grains with water.

12. Pour the soaked sunflower seed or grains and water into the basket to drain.

13. Tip the basket one way and then the other as the water drains for several minutes.

14. Place the basket into a completely enclosed clear tent.

15. The greenhouse can be set in an out-of-the-way location at room temperature for two or three days. The location of the greenhouse should be shaded, though it is not necessary that it is kept in the dark.

16. Keep your greenhouse watered during this period by giving your little sprouts good showers. The sprouts require more than a misting; they need a good rain. Do not use the hard run of a faucet, but employ a scattered shower. The goal here is to give them a good rinsing. (The only time your sprouts should be out of their greenhouse is when they are being watered.)

17. The greenhouse should remain in a shaded area for about four days.

18. After four days, place the greenhouse in a well-lit place in indirect sunlight for four or five days.

19. Water the greens daily during this period. Again, they require a hearty shower.

20. After the eighth day (four days of shade and four days of sun), you will

notice that your sprouts have rooted themselves in the basket. If you turn the basket upside down and brush it gently, the hulls will fall. You can even dip your basket in cool water to give the sprouts a bath.

21.   By the ninth day, you can harvest your garden.

22.   To harvest the greens, grab bunches of sprouts and gently wiggle them free of the basket. You will leave roots behind that can be cleaned out of the basket by cutting with a pair of scissors.

23.   Place the sprouts in a bowl of cool water to rinse. Move them around with your fingers to release the remaining hulls.

24.   Drain the sprouts in a colander.

25.   Allow the sprouts to dry for at least eight hours before you refrigerate them.

26.   Store the produce in a glass container in the refrigerator for up to two weeks, though it is best consumed as soon as possible.

The first part of this book has given you a guide to growing sprouts. The chapters to this point have outlined the anatomy of seeds, the equipment necessary to get you started and what you will need as you progress, the seeds that are good to start with, and various methods of sprouting those seeds. The wonderful thing about sprouts is that they are not only easy to grow and packed with vital nutritional benefits, but they are also a food that you can eat without further preparation. You can snack on sunflower sprouts like you snack on caramel corn. However, the upside to sprouts over something like caramel corn is that they are so much more versatile.

Now that you know how to properly grow your sprouts, you will want to use them however you can. What follows is the guide to using sprouts, including many easy-to-make recipes.

CASE STUDY: WOOD PRAIRIE FARM AND FAMILY GARDEN

Wood Prairie Farm and Family Garden
www.woodprairie.com

Megan and Jim Gerritsen own and operate Wood Prairie Farm and Family Garden in Bridgewater, Maine. They grow sprouts for their family table and sell them in their mail-order catalog at **www.woodprairie.com**. They have been growing sprouts for 25 years.

Megan Gerritsen said, "I love to have fresh greens on the table all year-round. Sprouts are the freshest greens available. We use the Sproutmaster sprouters because they take the guess work out of sprouting and ensure successful sprouting." (Note: The Sproutmaster is a stackable tray sprouter that is available at **www.sproutpeople.com/devices/sproutmaster/sm.html**.)

"We choose to eat all things organic, both sprouts and non-sprouts," Megan Gerritsen said. "We are certified organic farmers and just like to live as free of chemicals in as close a harmony with the earth's ecology and supporting other organic farmers as much as we can."

Gerritsen's advice to new sprouters is, "Mix your seeds. Variety is fun. Get started and keep going."

For the Gerritsens' delicious carrot and sprout salad recipe, turn to Chapter 7.

Chapter 6

Getting Started with Recipes: Snacks and Dips

The last chapter suggested you can eat sprouts as a snack, which is, perhaps, the best way to begin your experiment in cooking with and using sprouts. By eating sprouts unadorned, you will get a good sense of their flavor before you add them any dish. If you have never eaten a radish sprout, sit down and eat a small bowl of them with nothing on them. If you have never experienced the soft crunch of a soaked almond, try a small serving of them plain before you add them to a recipe that calls for soaked almonds.

Not only will eating these foods help you understand how they interact with the other ingredients in your recipe, they may also give you ideas of recipes of your own. You will start to think about taste combinations that are included here. Cooking this way demands a creative palate. As you learn to grow sprouts and learn more recipes that include them as ingredients, you will alter the recipes to match your own taste. Take note of what you enjoy and what does not work for you. Where one recipe calls for radish sprouts, you may find that arugula or onion works better. Remember that recipes are not written in stone so feel free to be creative and have fun.

You will find that many recipes call for sprouts to be used in combinations. This is something to consider as you grow sprouts and begin to experiment with both growing and eating sprouts. You will see recipes in the following pages that combine wheat sprouts with many other sprouts. Wheat combines in breads and cereals with chickpeas, lentils, rye, sunflower, and almonds. You will note that in soups, salads, and juices alfalfa often combines with lentil, wheat, cabbage, sunflower, mung bean, radish, rye, adzuki, and chickpea. Alfalfa is a very versatile sprout, as is wheat, so as you begin to consider what sprouts you should start with as you explore recipes, wheat and alfalfa sprouts are among the best choices.

Versatility is the word of the day when you begin to start thinking about sprout recipes. You can have sprouts at every meal of the day in many different ways. The recipes that follow will start by describing some uses for sprouts as snacks. From there, you will find recipes that you can use throughout the day as you explore recipes for everything including pancakes, cereals, sandwiches, soups, salads, casseroles, breads, and juices. You will enjoy sprouts in stir-fry, dip, dressings, and dessert. Not only will you enjoy sprouts, but your pets will reap the many health benefits of your home sprouting adventure.

There is at least one recipe for each type of sprout described in Chapter 4 of this book. In many cases, there are multiple recipes for a particular type of sprout. There are many recipes that employ wheat, alfalfa, and black turtle beans. There are some recipes that call for seeds to be used in ways other than sprouts. A good example is a recipe that calls for popped amaranth along with amaranth sprouts. The recipes are as much about fun as they are about nutrition and flavor. Have fun and experiment as you learn, cook, and, of course, eat.

Most of the recipes in this book are vegetarian, though there are a number of recipes that include meat or meat broth. Some recipes present both a meat and meatless version. If you see a recipe that looks intriguing that includes meat and you are a vegetarian, do not be afraid to try it without the meat. You can also substitute vegetable broth for chicken broth. *There is a good recipe for vegetable broth in Chapter 8.* Often, you can substitute a hardy sprouted grain such as barley for meat in many recipes. Do not fear experimentation.

The recipes included here are a good variety of some standard sprout-based recipes (such as the Asian sprout and noodle dish Pad Thai), some recipe that employ sprouts that will probably be completely new to you (such as the flourless Essene bread), and there are also recipes that are re-imagined in a new way to utilize the wonder of sprouts (such as lasagna). The hope is that you will enjoy them all and learn the most from the re-imagined recipes. Whether you are making pancakes, peanut butter sandwiches, meatloaf, or carrot cake, sprouts can be an enjoyable part of your everyday diet.

In the following recipes, the sprouts should all be grown according to directions given in the earlier chapters of this book, unless otherwise noted. Here again, as you proceed and learn more about your likes and dislikes, you may alter ways of sprouting for various recipes.

A final note before you proceed: Read a recipe all the way through before you begin to make the dish. Some recipe will call for you to begin several days in advance. Know and understand the requirements of each recipe prior to beginning.

Snacks are the best food items for experimentation because you can be as simple or as complex as you wish when you prepare sprouted snack items. The simple sprouted snack is simply eating the sprouts alone with no adornment. The following recipes offer several fun ways to prepare snacks that are a little more involved than just eating a handful of sprouts. They are all good and (be warned) very tasty.

Snackin' Sprouts

This is a recipe that is a good starting point for a multitude of variations. Rather than seasoning the sprouts with the onion powder, garlic powder, tamari, and cayenne as suggested, you might consider going a sweet route and adding a little sugar and cinnamon.

This recipe yields one to two servings.

Ingredients

1 cup of your favorite sprouts

2 Tbsp. onion powder

1 tsp. garlic powder

2 Tbsp. tamari (soy sauce)

¼ tsp. cayenne pepper

Directions

1. Preheat oven to 250 degrees.
2. Place sprouts in a mixing bowl.
3. Add 2 Tbsp. onion powder, 1 tsp. garlic powder, 2 Tbsp. tamari (soy sauce), and ¼ tsp. cayenne pepper.
4. Gently mix seasoning into sprouts.
5. Spread sprout mixture evenly on a baking sheet.
6. Bake at 250 degrees until crisp (this should take about one hour).
7. Remove from oven to cool.
8. Transfer to a glass jar or a container with a lid.

Extra Crunchy Peanut Butter Apples

If an apple with a dollop of peanut butter on it is not nutritious enough, you can make it even healthier by adding sunflower seed sprouts.

This recipe yields one serving.

Ingredients

One medium apple

2 Tbsp. peanut butter

2 Tbsp. sunflower seed sprouts

Directions

1. Wash and cut the apple in half.
2. Remove the core.
3. Fill the core of each half of the apple with 1 Tbsp. of sunflower seed sprouts.
4. Cover sunflower seed sprouts on each half with 1 Tbsp. of peanut butter.
5. Alternatively, you can use a celery rib in place of the apple.

Sprouted Stuffed Dates

This is similar to the recipe above, but takes a little more work. If you really like dates, this is quite addictive.

This recipe yields one serving.

Ingredients

6 Tbsp. sunflower seed sprouts

4 Tbsp. sesame seed sprouts

12 fresh dates

Honey

Directions

1. Place six of the dates in a blender or food processor.
2. Add sunflower seed sprouts and sesame seed sprouts and process on high until you have a paste.
3. Split the remaining dates in half and remove the pit.
4. Fill date halves with paste.
5. Place a dot of honey on top of each dollop of paste.

Sprouted Crackers

This sprouted seed cracker is very simple to make, and is wonderful as a snack or to use as an hors d'oeuvre. The crackers are crisp, flavorful, and sturdy enough to stand up to the thickest of dips. A selection of complementary dips is included after the cracker recipe.

This recipe yields about two dozen crackers.

Ingredients

1 cup stone-ground, whole-wheat flour

1 cup unbleached, all-purpose white flour

½ cup whole rye (pumpernickel) flour

½ cup whole yellow or white cornmeal

2 tsp. salt

2 Tbsp. olive oil

1 cup water

½ cup assorted seeds, such as poppy, fennel, caraway, and anise

½ cup sprouted sesame seeds

1 Tbsp. dried dill

1 Tbsp. dried tarragon

1 tsp. fresh ground black pepper

1 Tbsp. kosher salt (optional)

Directions

1. With the rack in the center position of the oven, preheat the oven to 450 degrees.
2. Line a baking sheet with parchment paper.
3. Sift together the flours, cornmeal, and salt into a food processor bowl fitted with the steel S-blade blade.
4. Pulse the olive oil thoroughly into the flour.
5. Add the water by pulsing it 2 Tbsp. at a time into the flour. (Your goal is to make a stiff dough ball so you may not need all of the water.) Add water until the dough is stiff, but not crumbly.
6. Turn the dough out onto a floured board and knead it until it is a stiff yet elastic ball of dough.
7. Combine the seeds, sprouts, herbs, pepper, and salt, if you are using it, in a small bowl.
8. Divide the dough into eight equal balls and cover them with plastic wrap. Work with one piece of dough at a time.
9. Scatter about 1 Tbsp. of the seed/sprout mixture on the work surface.
10. Press the dough onto the seed/sprout mixture.
11. Roll the dough out with a rolling pin to about ⅛ inch.
12. If the dough sticks, flip it over, apply more seeds, and continue rolling.
13. Place the rolled dough on the prepared baking sheet. You may have to use a spatula to get the dough off the rolling surface.
14. Bake the dough seven to ten minutes or until the cracker is slightly brown.
15. Cool completely on wire racks before serving.

Cream Cheese and Sprout Spread

Now that you have some wonderful fresh sprouted crackers, try this tasty cream cheese spread as a topping.

This recipe yields eight to 12 servings.

Ingredients

8 oz. cream cheese

½ cup chopped chives

1 tsp. horseradish mustard

½ tsp. salt

½ tsp. fresh ground pepper

¼ cup chopped alfalfa sprouts

¼ cup chopped radish sprouts

Directions

1. In a mixer, cream the cheese together with mustard and salt. To do this, place all the ingredients in the mixing bowl and mix until the cheese is soft and the ingredients are blended well together.
2. Add chives and sprouts.
3. Chill the mixture in the refrigerator for several hours and shape into a long log.
4. Lightly sprinkle fresh ground pepper on top of log.

Creamy Cucumber Sprout Spread

This recipe yields eight to 12 servings.

Ingredients

8 oz. cream cheese

1 cucumber

2 tsp. chive sprouts

½ cup chopped alfalfa sprouts

1 tsp. salt

Directions

1. Cut unpeeled cucumber in half lengthwise.
2. Scoop out seeds and center pulp of cucumber.
3. Coarsely shred remaining cucumber.
4. Drain shredded cucumber in a fine sieve or in cheesecloth.
5. Mix cucumber with cream cheese and sprouts.

Enjoy on sprouted crackers, Essene bread, or with your favorite vegetables.

Black Turtle Bean Dip

This dip yields six servings.

Ingredients

3 cups sprouted black turtle beans

3 small tomatoes

1 medium onion

1 tsp. cumin

¼ tsp. cayenne pepper

1 clove garlic

Directions

1. Cook black turtle bean sprouts by placing them in 6 to 8 cups water and bringing the water to a boil.
2. Reduce heat to a very slow simmer.

3.   Simmer for two hours.

4.   Drain black turtle bean sprouts.

5.   Place black turtle bean sprouts in a food processor.

6.   Add all remaining ingredients together.

7.   Process all ingredients until well mixed and smooth.

Sprouted Sunflower Seed and Cashew Dip

This is called a dip, but it is also a great spread for crackers and sandwiches. Try this tasty spread on the Sprouted Crackers mentioned earlier or Essene Bread (*Chapter 12*). Another wonderfully healthy way to enjoy this spread is to put it on a large spinach leaf with a slice of tomato and a slice of avocado. Wrap it all together and enjoy.

This recipe yields four servings.

Ingredients

1½ cups sprouted sunflower seeds

1 Tbsp. wheat germ

1¼ tsp. kosher salt

4 Tbsp. fresh lemon juice

½ finely chopped tart apple (Granny Smith)

1 finely chopped stalk celery

½ cup cashews

½ cup water

1 tsp. Dijon mustard

Dash of ground cardamom

Dash of cinnamon

Dash of cumin

Dash of ground cloves

Dash of fresh ground black pepper

Dash of nutmeg

Directions

1. Place sunflower seed sprouts, wheat germ, 1 tsp. kosher salt, and 2 Tbsp. lemon juice into a food processor bowl.
2. Pulse sunflower seed mixture five times for five seconds each pulse, scraping the bowl between pulses.
3. Transfer sprouted sunflower seed mixture to a mixing bowl.
4. Add apple and celery to sunflower seed mixture and mix well.
5. Set sprouted sunflower seed mixture aside.
6. Combine the cashews, water, Dijon mustard, ¼ tsp. kosher salt, cardamom, cinnamon, cumin, ground cloves, black pepper, and nutmeg.
7. Blend all ingredients on high speed until well blended and creamy.
8. Add the cashew mix from the blender to the sprouted sunflower seed mixture and mix well.

Sprouted Guacamole

This dip can also be a spread or a salad dressing. Guacamole is another dish that can be made various ways to suit many different purposes and tastes. This recipe is just a starting point for your imagination. The first six ingredients listed below will give you a very basic guacamole and the rest of the ingredients are optional and can be substituted with a huge variety of ingredients to suit your tastes.

The serving suggestions for guacamole range from a dip for corn or potato chips, a spread for burritos, a topper for baked potatoes, or a sandwich spread topped with tomatoes, spinach, and a mountain of sprouts.

This recipe yields four servings.

Ingredients

2 mashed ripe avocados

1 lemon, juiced

2 to 3 crushed cloves of garlic

1 tsp. salt

Chili powder (to taste)

Fresh ground black pepper (to taste)

3 finely chopped scallions

1 finely chopped hard-boiled egg

Directions

1. Cut the avocados in half and remove the peel and the pit.
2. Put the avocados in a food processor with the lemon juice, garlic, salt, chili powder, and fresh ground black pepper.
3. Add mayonnaise, sour cream, or yogurt if desired.
4. Run food processor until avocado mixture is smooth and creamy.
5. Add scallions, hard-boiled egg, alfalfa sprouts, and radish sprouts to food processor.
6. Pulse food processor to bring guacamole to desired consistency.

Sprouted Chickpea and Parsley Dip

Because it contains chickpeas and tahini, this recipe can be considered hummus. To make a more traditional hummus, you can leave out the parsley and green onions. If you sprout the chickpeas right before you make this recipe, you can use the soak water as the water in the recipe.

This recipe yields four servings.

Ingredients

2 cups sprouted chickpeas

¼ cup water

1 clove garlic

3 Tbsp. lemon juice

⅓ cup tahini 2 chopped green onions

½ tsp. ground cumin

¼ tsp. soy sauce

½ cup chopped parsley

¼ tsp. cayenne pepper

Salt (to taste)

Fresh ground black pepper (to taste)

Directions

1. Combine chickpeas, water, garlic, lemon juice, tahini, green onions, cumin, soy sauce, and parsley in a food processor.
2. Process ingredients until smooth.
3. Season to taste with cayenne, salt, and fresh ground black pepper.

Serve on pita bread or on sprouted crackers.

Spicey Sprouted Hummus

Because it contains chickpeas and tahini, this recipe can also be considered hummus.

This recipe yields four servings.

Ingredients

1 cup sprouted chickpeas

½ cup soaked sunflower or pumpkin seeds

Juice of 1 lemon

2 crushed garlic cloves

1 cup fresh chopped parsley

2 Tbsp. olive oil

1 tsp. kosher salt

A pinch of ground cayenne pepper

Soy sauce (optional)

Directions

1. Put sprouted chickpeas and soaked sunflower or pumpkin seeds into the bowl of a food processor.

2. Process the sprouted chickpeas and soaked sunflower or pumpkin seeds to a pasty consistency.

3. Add olive oil, the juice of one lemon, and the crushed garlic cloves to food processor and process for about 30 seconds.

4. Add ½ cup of finely chopped fresh parsley and pulse five times. (You just want to lightly incorporate this into the mix.)

5. Add salt and cayenne pepper to food processor and pulse five times.

6. Add soy sauce if you desire and pulse five times.

Serve with cut-up vegetables, sprouted crackers, pita, or thyme and sprouted sesame bread.

Baba Ghanouj

Here is a sprouted adaptation of a wonderful traditional Middle Eastern recipe for baba ghanouj, a chunky but light dip or spread that goes well with sprouted pita or sprouted crackers.

This recipe yields four to six servings.

Ingredients

3 Tbsp. olive oil

2 medium eggplants

½ cup pine nuts

¼ cup fresh squeezed lemon juice (may use up to ½ cup lemon juice
    to taste)

⅓ cup tahini

2 crushed garlic cloves

1 tsp. ground cumin

½ tsp. salt

¼ tsp. cayenne pepper

½ cup sprouted sesame seeds

4 Tbsp. chopped fresh cilantro

Directions

1. Preheat oven to 375 degrees.
2. Generously oil rimmed baking sheet.
3. Rub 1 Tbsp. olive oil over the two eggplants and slice the egg-plants in half length-wise.
4. Place eggplant halves, cut side down, on baking sheet.
5. Roast, turning once or twice, about 45 minutes, or until eggplant is very soft.
6. Remove eggplant from oven and allow to cool slightly.
7. Spoon pulp from eggplant and put it into a colander set over a bowl.
8. Let the eggplant sit in the colander for about 30 minutes to allow excess liquid to drain away.
9. Transfer eggplant pulp to a food processor.
10. Add 2 Tbsp. olive oil, pine nuts, tahini, lemon juice, garlic, ground cumin, salt, and cayenne pepper to food processor.
11. Process mixture until almost smooth.
12. Season to taste with additional salt and pepper.
13. Transfer mixture to small bowl.
14. Add and stir in sprouted sesame seeds and chopped cilantro.

You can make this one day ahead of time, though it is best as fresh as possible. To store this dish, cover and chill in the refrigerator. Bring to room temperature before serving.

Nut Pâté

This recipe yields eight servings.

Ingredients

1 cup soaked almonds

1 cup soaked pumpkin seeds

1 cup sprouted sunflower seeds

¼ cup sprouted sesame seeds

3 stalks finely chopped celery

1 finely chopped leek

1 finely chopped red bell pepper

2 Tbsp. lemon juice

Directions

1. Place soaked almonds in a bowl and cover the almonds with boiling water.

2. Allow the almonds sit in hot water for only one minute.

3. Drain almonds and rinse them under cold water.

4. Allow almonds to drain.

5. Place soaked almonds, soaked pumpkin seeds, sprouted sunflower seeds, and sprouted sesame seeds in the bowl of a food processor.

6. Process mixture until smooth.

7. Transfer mixture to a mixing bowl.

8. Add remaining ingredients to mixing bowl and mix well.

9. Serve as a spread for sprouted crackers, Essene bread, or fresh raw vegetables.

Nutloaf

This recipe yields eight servings.

Ingredients

1 cup soaked almonds

1 cup soaked hazelnuts (Soak the hazelnuts the same way that you soak the almonds.)

1 cup sprouted sunflower seeds

1-inch piece fresh ginger, grated

4 finely chopped stalks celery

1 finely grated medium carrot

1 finely chopped red bell pepper

1 finely grated zucchini

¼ cup finely chopped parsley

1 tsp. dried marjoram

½ tsp. coriander

Directions

1. Place soaked almonds in a bowl and cover with boiling water.
2. Allow the almonds sit in hot water for only one minute.
3. Drain almonds and then rinse the almonds under cold water.
4. Allow almonds to drain.
5. Place soaked almonds, soaked hazelnuts, sprouted sunflower seeds, and grated ginger in the bowl of a food processor.
6. Process ingredients until they are mixed well but not quite a smooth paste.
7. Transfer mixture to a mixing bowl.
8. Add remaining ingredients to mixing bowl and mix well.
9. Form into a nut loaf.
10. Refrigerate for at least one hour.

Serve on a plate surrounded by your favorite sprouts as a spread for sprouted crackers, Essene bread, or fresh raw vegetables.

Sun-dried Tomato Nut Pâté

This yields four servings.

Ingredients

¼ cup soaked cashew spread (see directions below)

½ cup soaked almonds

½ cup sprouted sunflower seeds

2 tsp. olive oil

1 Tbsp. minced onion

2 Tbsp. minced fresh basil

2 oz. soft goat cheese

3 oz. oil-packed sun-dried tomatoes, with excess oil squeezed off

⅛ tsp. dried thyme

Salt (to taste)

For soaked cashew spread

Ingredients

¼ cup raw cashews soaked for four to six hours

1 tsp. fresh squeezed lemon juice

¼ tsp. salt

2 tsp. water

Directions

1. Place soaked cashews, lemon juice, salt, and 1 tsp. of the water in the bowl of a food processor.

2. Pulse ten to 15 times to blend the mixture until it reaches the texture of ricotta cheese.

3. Add more water as needed.

4. Set mixture aside in a small bowl.

For the sun-dried tomato nut pate

Directions:

1. Place the soaked cashew spread, soaked almonds, sprouted sunflower seeds, olive oil, minced onion, minced basil, goat cheese, sun-dried tomatoes, dried thyme, and salt in the bowl of a food processor.

2. Process the mixture until smooth.

3. Stir in additional herbs if desired.

Serve on a plate surrounded by your favorite sprouts as a spread for sprouted crackers, Essene bread, or fresh raw vegetables

As you continue exploring recipes that employ sprouts and begin to experiment with the sprout salads in the following chapter, consider combining some of the recipes of this chapter, particularly the dip recipes, to complement the salads.

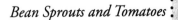

Bean Sprouts and Tomatoes

CASE STUDY:JEANNE GRUNERT

Jeanne Grunert
Seven Oaks Consulting
www.sevenoaksconsulting.com

Jeanne Grunert has been sprouting for personal use since around 2002.

Grunert said, "I believe sprouts are a very healthy addition to the diet. Many sprouts are rich in vitamins, minerals, and enzymes. They're inexpensive and tasty too!"

She considers the enzymes the greatest health benefit to growing and consuming sprouts. The said these enzymes are considered the life-giving force from raw foods.

Grunert uses a two-tray home sprouter kit called The Kitchen Sprouter that she purchased from the Parks Seed company several years ago. She said you can use any recycled container to start sprouts, including mason jars or plastic containers, because the sprouts "aren't fussy." She enjoys sprouting mung beans, alfalfa, broccoli, and a salad mix. Among those, mung beans were the easiest to sprout, followed by the alfalfa and broccoli. She said, "As long as I follow general sprouting guidelines and purchase seeds especially for sprouting, I'd try anything."

"To me, organic would have to include non-genetically modified (GMO). Organic should mean seeds raised without pesticides and also non-GMO. Genetically modified is, I think, worse in the long run than conventional seeds. With GMO seeds, we may be doing untold damage to our intestinal floral and fauna," Grunert said.

Grunert suggests that those who are new to sprouting should jump in and try different things. She said, "It's fun to start. Don't sprout too many seeds at once because they don't store well. Do a little at a time, and enjoy them. You can eat them in many yummy ways. Pile them on sandwiches, or add them to salads or even stir-fries. Just start with whatever you have and wherever you are at. It's really fun and tasty too. I usually make a salad of lemon juice, cold pressed olive oil, and sea salt. It's simply delicious! I also like to add alfalfa sprouts to tuna fish salad sandwiches.

Chapter 7

Salads and Dressings

There are endless combinations of sprouts, shoots, greens, fruits, nuts, and seeds that you can use to make an array of salads. Here are recipes to get you started and to get your creative salad juices flowing. In some cases there are no amounts given for items such as greens, sprouts, and other ingredients because the amounts will be determined by the number of people you are feeding and your own tastes.

The first recipe included here was submitted by one of this book's case studies (*Chapter 5*), Megan Gerritsen of Wood Prairie Farm.

Carrot and Sprout Salad

This recipe yields two serving.

Ingredients

Two large Chantenay carrots (This is a thick, red-cored variety of carrot. If you cannot find them in your grocery store, you might try growing them. Seeds are available at **www.woodprairie.com**.)

Alfalfa or clover sprouts

Radish sprouts

Lentil or pea sprouts

¼ cup raisins

Directions

1. Coarsely grate two large Chantenay carrots.
2. Arrange the carrots in the bottom of a shallow salad bowl.
3. On top of the carrots, add a variety of sprouts: mild clover or alfalfa, a few hot radish sprouts, and some nutty lentil or pea sprouts.
4. Top with ¼ cup of raisins.

Dress with ginger garlic salad dressing.

Mixed Vegetable Salad

Garlic Ginger Salad Dressing

Ingredients

¼ cup olive or sunflower oil

2 Tbsp. cider vinegar

1 Tbsp. tamari (soy sauce)

1 Tbsp. maple syrup

1 clove garlic

½ inch of organic ginger

½ tsp. salt

¼ tsp. pepper

1 tsp. tahini

Directions

1. In food processor, combine olive or sunflower oil, cider vinegar, tamari, maple syrup, garlic, organic ginger, salt, and pepper. Peel the garlic and the ginger before adding them to the food processor.
2. Blend well until smooth.
3. Add 1 tsp. of tahini for a richer dressing.

Mixed Green Salad with Sweet and Sour Dressing

Ingredients

Mesclun salad mix (This is a mixture of young salad greens.)

Flat leaf parsley

Greened sprouts/shoots such as alfalfa, cabbage, fenugreek, radish (A good amount of sprouts to use is one part sprouts to four parts salad mix.)

Note: The amounts of the above ingredients will be determined by taste and volume needed.

Directions

1. Toss all ingredients together in a bowl.
2. Dress with sweet and sour dressing.

For Dressing

Ingredients

1 part balsamic vinegar

1 part rice syrup or honey

4 parts olive oil

Salt to taste

Directions

1. Mix balsamic vinegar and rice syrup or honey together in a bowl with a whisk.
2. Whisk in olive oil.
3. Add salt to taste.

Crazy for Radish Salad

Like so many other salads, the fresher the produce you use, the more likely you are to have a tasty dish. In the case of this simple salad, because you are using fresh radish sprouts, make sure that the radishes you use are as fresh as possible. You can add a little feta cheese to the top of this salad for even more flavor.

This recipe yields four servings.

Ingredients

4 cups thinly sliced radishes

1 cup radish sprouts

3 Tbsp. red wine vinegar or lemon juice

1 tsp. sugar or honey

1 Tbsp. salt

Fresh ground pepper to taste

Directions

1. Combine vinegar, sugar, and salt with a whisk.
2. Toss radishes with vinegar mixture.
3. Marinate in refrigerator for one to two hours.
4. Drain marinade off the radishes.
5. Top with radish sprouts when serving. Add salt and pepper to taste.

Sprouted Arugula Salad ————————————•

This recipe yields four servings.

Ingredients

¼ lb. arugula, washed, trimmed, and dried off

1 cup arugula sprouts

1 cup sesame sprouts

1 to 2 small tomatoes, rinsed and diced

1 avocado, cubed

1 cup or more soaked almonds

¼ lb. spinach

1 lemon, zested and juiced (To zest the lemon, gently scrape off the
   yellow of the rind with a grater. The yellow part of the rind is the
   zest.)

Apple juice or other available sweet juice (to taste)

Extra virgin olive oil (to taste)

Salt (to taste)

Directions

1. Make the vinaigrette by combining the lemon zest, lemon juice,
    apple juice, and olive oil. (Everything is to taste depending on
    how sweet or sour you like your dressing. A good rule of thumb is
    to use about three times as much oil as vinegar.)

2. Salt vinaigrette to taste.

3. In a large bowl, gently toss the all ingredients, making sure not to
    bruise or smash anything. (Because the avocados are particularly
    tender, you might choose to add in the nuts and cubed avocado
    at the end.)

4. Chill for one hour.

Fenugreek Sprout Salad

This recipe yields two servings.

Ingredients

1 cup fenugreek sprouts

4 green onions

1 finely chopped tomato

1 finely chopped carrot

1 finely chopped cucumber

1 pressed garlic clove

1 Tbsp. olive oil

1 Tbsp. finely chopped coriander leaves

½ finely chopped small green chili pepper

½ cup chopped sprouted peanuts

½ cup popped amaranth

1 tsp. sweet tamarind chutney

½ tsp. lemon juice

Salt (to taste)

Directions

1. Crush garlic into a small bowl with olive oil.
2. Rub garlic and olive oil over the inside of a large wooden salad bowl to coat the bowl.
3. In the bowl, toss together sprouts, green onion, tomato, carrot, and cucumber.
4. Add chutney, green chili pepper, lemon juice, and salt just before serving.
5. Toss well to blend flavor.
6. Add in half of the popped amaranth and coriander leaves and toss lightly.

7. Spoon into individual serving bowls.
8. Garnish with chopped sprouted peanuts and remaining popped amaranth and serve immediately.

Mung Bean Sprout Salad

This is a tasty, warm salaf that is very is to prepare. This recipe yields four servings.

Ingredients

3 Tbsp. peanut oil

¼ cup pine nuts

1 lb. fresh bean sprouts

1 red bell pepper cut in small strips

1 tsp. salt

½ tsp. sugar

2 tsp. white vinegar

Directions

1. In a wok over a medium-high heat, heat oil until it just begins to smoke.
2. Add pine nuts and stir fry for one minute.
3. Remove the wok from the heat and allow it to cool for about three minutes.
4. Remove the pine nuts from the wok, leaving the oil behind.
5. Heat oil in wok over medium-high heat until it just begins to smoke.
6. Add sprouts and red peppers and stir fry for one minute.
7. Add remaining ingredients (including pine nuts) to the wok.
8. Toss all ingredients together.

9. Serve warm or you may allow the mixture to cool and serve chilled.

Red Cabbage and Adzuki Sprout Salad

This recipe yields eight servings.

Salad Ingredients

1 large red cabbage

1 small red bell pepper, de-seeded and diced

½ small pineapple, peeled and finely chopped (You can also use 1 cup frozen pineapple chunks or 1 cup of canned pineapple chunks.)

2 oranges, peeled and segmented

6 green onions, thinly sliced

3 celery ribs and leaves, chopped

½ cup soaked almonds (*See Chapter 4 for directions on soaking almonds.*)

½ cup adzuki bean sprouts (*See Chapter 4 for directions on sprouting adzuki beans.*)

Dressing Ingredients

½ cup plain yogurt

¼ cup mayonnaise

1 Tbsp. freshly squeezed orange juice

Salt (to taste)

Fresh ground black pepper (to taste)

Directions

1. Clean cabbage by removing the outer discolored or tough leaves.
2. Cut the base of the cabbage head to remove the stalk.
3. Finely shred the cabbage.

4. Put the shredded cabbage into a large bowl.
5. Add the red bell pepper, pineapple, orange segments, green onions, celery and leaves, soaked almonds, and sprouted adzuki beans to the large bowl.
6. In a separate bowl, whisk together yogurt, mayonnaise, and orange juice.
7. Gently fold in the dressing with the cabbage mixture.
8. Cover and chill for one hour before serving.

Brassica Sprout Slaw

Brassica is a genus of plants in the mustard family. Some members of this family include cabbage, Brussels sprouts, cauliflower, and broccoli.

This slaw recipe yields two to four servings.

Ingredients

1 cup cabbage sprouts
1 cup broccoli sprouts
½ cup fresh chopped pineapple
½ cup raisins
½ cup non-fat yogurt
¼ cup mayonnaise
1 tsp. Dijon mustard
Salt (to taste)

Directions
1. Mix sprouts and fruit in a large bowl.
2. Whisk raisins, yogurt, mayonnaise, and Dijon mustard together in a separate bowl.
3. Add whisked ingredients to sprouts and fruit by gently stirring into the large bowl.

4. Chill for one hour.

Serve over spinach or other greens.

Mexican Sprout Slaw

This recipe yields four to six servings.

Ingredients

For the slaw

3 cups of your favorite loosely packed mixed sprouts

1 cup loosely packed shredded purple cabbage

½ cup loosely packed shredded carrot

½ cup lightly toasted pumpkin seeds

For the dressing

¼ cup pumpkin seed oil

2 Tbsp. fresh lime juice

1 Tbsp. apple cider vinegar

1 Tbsp. dried oregano

1 tsp. coarse salt

½ tsp. fresh ground black pepper

Directions

1. Combine all slaw ingredients in a salad bowl and toss them together well.
2. Combine all dressing ingredients in a small bowl and use a whisk to mix them together well.
3. Toss dressing in bowl with slaw.
4. Top with toasted pumpkin seeds and serve.

Spinach, Pea, and Onion Sprout Salad

This recipe yields four servings.

Salad Ingredients
6 cups washed and patted dry baby spinach leaves

1 cup onion sprouts

1 cup pea sprouts

Dressing Ingredients
⅓ cup fresh lime juice

⅓ cup soy sauce

4 Tbsp. honey

1 minced jalapeno chili pepper

2 minced garlic cloves

2 Tbsp. canola oil

Directions
1. Place spinach, pea sprouts, and onion sprouts in a large salad bowl.
2. Place all dressing ingredients in a food processor with a stainless steel S-blade.
3. Pulse ingredients briefly to combine, but be sure to leave a little chunk in the liquid.
4. Toss dressing with salad ingredients.

This is a wonderful recipe that you can really brag about if you include your own sprouts and homemade farmer's cheese. If you are not up to making the cheese, you can substitute cottage cheese.

Farmer's Cheese and Fruit Salad

This yields four to six servings.

For the farmer's cheese

Ingredients

1 quart farm-fresh milk (or whole milk that still has the cream on top)
Salt (optional)
Homemade butter (optional)

Directions

1. In a glass container, allow milk to ripen in a warm place, though out of the sun, for 24 hours. Room temperature or warmer, though not hot, is fine for this.
2. Pour ripened milk into the stainless steel pot of a double boiler.
3. Gently heat milk until the curds and whey separate.
4. Line a colander with a large doubled piece of cheesecloth. Make sure the cloth is large enough that you will be able to bring the corners together in a bag for the cheese to drain. Place the colander over a pot to catch the whey.
5. Gently pour the curds into the cheesecloth-lined colander and allow the curds to drain for about ten minutes.
6. Bring and tie corners of cheesecloth together to form a bag and hang the bag over a pot.
7. Allow to drain for about four hours or until desired consistency is reached.
8. Salt to taste if desired.
9. Add butter and work it in with a wooden spoon if desired.

This cheese can be refrigerated in a sealed container for up to a week.

For the salad

Ingredients

½ cup honey

1 tsp. grated lemon zest (Make sure to use only the zest and not the
   pith, which is the white substance between the peel and the fruit.)

¼ cup fresh squeezed lemon juice

¼ tsp. dry mustard

Pinch of salt

1 lb. homemade cottage cheese or farmer's cheese

½ cup peeled and shredded carrots

¼ cup seedless raisins

¼ cup heavy cream (optional)

Lettuce leaves

1 small melon of your choice, halved, seeded, peeled, and sliced into
   wedges

1 kiwi, pared and sliced

Assortment of seedless grape varieties

1 cup strawberries, sliced

½ cup cress or clover sprouts, chopped.

Directions

1. For a dressing, whisk together honey, lemon zest, lemon juice, dry
    mustard, and salt.

2. Cover dressing and set aside, but do not refrigerate.

3. In a glass or food grade plastic bowl, combine cheese, carrots, and
    raisins.

4. Cover fruit and cheese. Chill until ready to serve.

5. Just prior to serving, arrange a bed of lettuce on a serving plate.

6. If you desire a creamier cheese and fruit mixture, gently stir the
    cream into the cheese and fruit.

7. Spoon and arrange cheese and fruit mixture onto lettuce bed.

8. Arrange additional fruit around cheese.

Wild Rice Salad

This recipe yields six to eight servings.

Ingredients

4 cups sprouted wild rice (Soak rice in water for two days. Change water after first day.)

½ cucumber

1 cup sprouted adzuki beans

1 cup chopped red bell pepper

½ cup shredded carrot

1 chopped medium tomato

1 chopped celery stalk

½ cup chopped sweet red onion or scallions

1 to 2 tsp. dried parsley or basil

1 mashed large avocado

½ to 1 cup tomato juice

1 to 3 crushed garlic cloves

Cayenne pepper (to taste)

1 cup alfalfa sprouts

Directions

1. Place wild rice in a large bowl.

2. Add adzuki beans, red bell pepper, carrot, tomato, celery, sweet red onion and dried parsley, to wild rice.

3. Toss ingredients in bowl and set aside.

4. Fold tomato juice, crushed garlic, and cayenne pepper into mashed avocado.

5.   Pour avocado mixture over wild rice mixture.

6.   Place in individual salad bowls and top with alfalfa sprouts.

It is quite easy to experiment with a large variety of sprouts for any of the recipes given in this chapter. Salads are wonderful this way, as are the soup recipes you will find in the following chapter. Do not be afraid to mix, match, or substitute your favorite sprouts in any of the recipes in this book.

Chapter 8

Soups, Stews, and Chili

Soup recipes are another invitation to play with your favorite ingredients. The basic idea of soup is to throw a bunch of ingredients into a pot with some liquid and cook it until it reaches the desired flavor. Soups and stews are simple comfort foods made to warm cold winter days, or, in the case of cold soups like gazpacho, refresh on those hot summer nights.

Vegetable Stew with Sprouted Quinoa

This recipe yields four to six serving.

Ingredients

½ cup quinoa

1 cup water

2 cups chopped onions

2 garlic cloves, minced or pressed

1 Tbsp. vegetable oil

1 celery stalk, chopped

1 carrot, cut on the diagonal into ¼-inch thick slices

1 red bell pepper, cut into 1-inch pieces

1 cup cubed sweet potatoes

½ cup corn, fresh or frozen then thawed

2 cups finely chopped fresh or canned tomatoes, undrained

1 cup vegetable stock 1 cup vegetable stock

2 tsp. ground cumin

½ tsp. chili powder

1 tsp. ground coriander

Pinch of cayenne (or more to taste)

2 tsp. fresh oregano or 1 tsp. dried oregano

Salt (to taste)

Chopped fresh cilantro (optional)

Grated hard white cheese (optional)

Directions

1. Place sprouted quinoa and water in pot and cover.
2. Cook on medium-low heat for about ten minutes until soft.
3. Place the onions, garlic, and vegetable oil in skillet and sauté on medium heat, stirring frequently, until onions are soft.
4. Add celery and carrots to the skillet and sauté an additional five minutes, stirring frequently.
5. Transfer sautéed vegetables to a soup pot.
6. Add red bell pepper, sweet potatoes, corn, tomatoes, and vegetable stock to soup pot.
7. Add cumin, chili powder, coriander, cayenne, and oregano to soup pot.
8. Simmer covered for 20 minutes until sweet potatoes are tender.
9. Stir in sprouted quinoa.
10. Salt to taste.
11. Top with a grated hard white cheese such as Parmesan or chopped cilantro.

Black Turtle Bean Soup

This recipe yields ten servings.

Ingredients

8 cups black turtle bean sprouts

1 gallon water

1½ Tbsp. cumin powder

2 tsp. dried oregano

2 tsp. ground black pepper

2 tsp. dried thyme

2 cups diced red onion

2 cups chopped celery

2 cups chopped carrots

2 Tbsp. minced garlic

4 Tbsp. olive oil

⅓ cup dry sherry

Salt (to taste)

Sharp cheddar cheese (grated)

Sour cream (to taste)

Directions

1. Place black turtle bean sprouts in a pot with 1 gallon cold water.
2. Add cumin, oregano, black pepper, and thyme to the pot.
3. Bring water to a boil then reduce to a very gentle simmer.
4. Allow mixture to simmer for one hour.
5. Sauté onions, celery, carrots, and garlic in olive oil until they are tender.
6. Add sautéed vegetables, sherry, and salt to black turtle bean sprouts after they have simmered for one hour.
7. Continue to simmer for one hour (a total cooking time of two hours).

8. Stir gently from bottom up to keep black turtle bean sprouts on bottom from sticking or burning.

Serve over rice with grated cheddar cheese and a dollop of sour cream on top.

Sprouted Black Bean Chili

This recipe yields four to six servings.

Ingredients

For the chili

2 cups finely chopped red onion

3 crushed garlic cloves

½ cup of water

1 Tbsp. ground cumin

1 Tbsp. ground coriander

1 cup salsa (see recipe below)

1 chopped green bell pepper

1 chopped red bell pepper

2½ cups cooked sprouted black beans (see directions below)

1 28-oz. can whole tomatoes with juice

2 cups corn (yellow or white corn, fresh or frozen)

Salt (to taste)

Hot pepper sauce (to taste)

¼ cup chopped fresh cilantrov

For the salsa

1 large finely chopped tomato

8 to 10 finely chopped tomatillos

¼ cup freshly chopped cilantro

¼ cup tomato juice

2 Tbsp. finely chopped jalapeno pepper

2 tsp. crushed garlic, minced

1 Tbsp. lime juice

¼ tsp. chili powder

¼ tsp. ground cumin

Salt (to taste)

Fresh ground black pepper (to taste)

1 finely chopped red bell pepper

1 finely chopped green bell pepper

⅓ cup chopped scallions

Directions

For salsa

1. Place the chopped tomato, chopped tomatillos, cilantro, tomato juice, jalapeno peppers, crushed garlic, lime juice, chili powder, ground cumin, salt, and pepper in the bowl of a food processor.
2. Pulse the ingredients in the food processor until they are at a desired consistency.

For cooking sprouted black beans

1. Put 4 cups of water and 1¼ cups of sprouted black beans in a large pot and bring the water to a boil.
2. Reduce water to a simmer.
3. Cook sprouted black beans for about ten minutes until soft.
4. Drain beans in a colander.

This recipe yields about 2½ cups.

For chili

1. Put the chopped onions, crushed garlic, and water in a soup pot and place the pot over medium-high heat.
2. Cover the pot.
3. Cook onions, garlic, and water for about five minutes, stirring frequently.
4. Stir cumin and coriander into soup pot
5. Cover and cook soup for another minute.
6. Stir salsa, red, and green bell peppers into chili.
7. Cover the pot and reduce the heat to medium low.
8. Simmer chili for five minutes, stirring occasionally.
9. Stir tomatoes with the juice from the tomatoes and sprouted black beans into chili.
10. Simmer chili for 15 minutes.
11. Stir corn into chili.
12. Simmer chili for 15 minutes.
13. Add salt and hot pepper sauce to taste.
14. Stir in cilantro just prior to serving.

Serve hot over rice (if desired) with corn chips.

Pumpkin Black Bean Soup

The following two recipes are very similar in nature in that they combine pumpkin and sprouted black beans. They both use meat (ham in the first and turkey in the second) though they can both be made without the meat. The first recipe falls into the soup category, as it is quite mild. The second recipe is a chili recipe that is thicker and spicier than the soup.

This recipe yields four to six servings.

Ingredients

3 cups of sprouted and cooked black beans

1 16-oz. can diced tomatoes

4 Tbsp. butter

1¼ cups chopped yellow onion

4 cloves crushed garlic

1 tsp. salt

½ tsp. fresh ground black pepper

4 cups beef broth

2 cups pumpkin puree (or 1 15-oz. can of pumpkin)

½ lb. cubed cooked ham

3 Tbsp. sherry vinegar

Sour cream

Directions

For cooking sprouted black beans

1. Put 5 cups of water and 1½ cups of sprouted black beans in a large pot.
2. Bring water and beans to a boil.
3. Reduce water to a simmer.
4. Cook sprouted black beans for about ten minutes until soft.
5. Drain beans in a colander.

This recipe yields about 3 cups

For cooking sprouted black beans

The ideal pumpkin to use for this (or any recipe you use to make pumpkin soup, chili, pie, or bread) is a sugar pumpkin. Sugar pumpkins are the smaller pumpkins you can purchase in stores or farmer's markets in the late summer and fall, as opposed to the larger jack-o-lantern pumpkins you might carve for Halloween.

1.   Preheat oven to 350 degrees.

2.   Slice the pumpkin in half around the middle. Clean the seeds and stringy inside out of the pumpkin. You may retain the seeds to toast or sprout.

3.   Lightly grease a baking pan or a large baking sheet (make sure the baking sheet has a raised edge or the juice from the pumpkin will run all over your oven).

4.   Place the two pumpkin halves cut side down on the greased baking pan and place them in the oven.

5.   Bake for one hour or until soft to the touch. (If the shell of the pumpkin is particularly hard, you may have to lift the hot pumpkin and check the inside of the pumpkin to see if it is cooked.)

6.   Remove the pumpkin from the oven and allow it to cool for about an hour.

7.   Scoop the pulp of the pumpkin from the inside of the shell.

8.   Discard the shell.

9.   Place the pumpkin pulp in the bowl of a food processor and process for about two minutes or until smooth.

One sugar pumpkin will yield about 2 cups of purred pumpkin.

For the soup

1.   Put 2 cups of the cooked and sprouted black beans and the can of diced tomatoes into the bowl a food processor and puree until smooth.

2.   Set the pureed sprouted black bean and tomatoes aside.

3.   Melt butter in a medium soup pot over medium heat.

4.   Add the onion, crushed garlic, salt, and fresh ground black pepper to the soup pot.

5.   Cook and stir the onion and crushed garlic until the onion is softened.

6. Stir the bean puree into the onion and crushed garlic mixture.

7. Add the remaining beans, beef broth, pumpkin puree, and sherry vinegar to the soup pot and mix until it is well blended.

8. Bring to soup to a low boil over a medium-high heat.

9. Reduce heat to medium low.

10. Simmer soup for about 30 to 45 minutes, or until thick enough to coat the back of a metal spoon.

11. Stir the cubed ham into the soup and simmer for another 15 minutes.

12. Serve hot in individual soup bowls with a dollop of sour cream.

Pumpkin Black Bean Chili

This recipe yields six to eight servings.

Ingredients

2 Tbsp. olive oil

1 chopped medium red onion

1 chopped red bell pepper

3 crushed garlic cloves

3 cups chicken broth (or water)

3 cups of sprouted and cooked black beans (See directions for cooking in previous recipe.)

2 cups pumpkin puree (or 1 15-oz. can of pumpkin) (See recipe for cooking and pureeing pumpkin in previous recipe.)

1 16-oz. can diced tomatoes, undrained

2 tsp. dried parsley flakes

2 tsp. chili powder

Hot red pepper (to taste)

1½ tsp. dried oregano

1½ tsp. ground cumin

½ tsp. salt

2½ cups cubed cooked turkey

¼ cup fine corn meal

¼ cup warm water

Directions

1. Pour olive oil into a large soup pot and heat over a medium-high heat.

2. Add the chopped red onion, chopped red bell pepper, and crushed garlic to the oil and sauté until tender.

3. Add remainder of ingredients except for cubed cooked turkey, corn meal, and ¼ cup warm water and heat over a medium-high heat until the ingredients reach a low boil.

4. Reduce heat to medium low and simmer, covered, for 45 minutes to an hour. Stir occasionally while simmering.

5. After the chili simmers for 45 minutes to an hour, add cubed cooked turkey.

6. Stir ¼ cup warm water into corn meal to make a thick paste.

7. Stir corn meal paste into chili.

8. Continue to simmer chili for about 15 minutes.

Serve chili hot with rice, a dollop of sour cream, and corn chips.

Green Pea Soup with Pea Sprouts

This recipe yields eight servings.

Ingredients

1 lb. ham bone

4½ cups water

2 cups chicken stock

2 cups dried split peas, rinsed

⅔ cups finely white onions

½ cup finely chopped carrots

⅓ cup finely chopped celery

2 cloves sliced garlic

2 bay leaves

½ tsp. sugar

⅛ tsp. crushed marjoram

⅛ tsp. freshly ground black pepper

2½ cups whole milk

1 cup heavy cream

¾ cup finely chopped cooked ham

Pea sprouts (to taste)

Sour cream (to taste)

Directions

1. In large soup pot or Dutch oven, combine ham bone, water, chicken stock, and split peas.
2. Bring to a boil over medium heat, occasionally skimming froth from the surface.
3. Reduce heat and simmer for 30 minutes.
4. Add white onions, carrots, celery, garlic, bay leaves, sugar, marjoram, and pepper.
5. Simmer, stirring occasionally, for 30 minutes to an hour until peas are soft.
6. Remove ham bone and gradually stir in milk and cream.
7. You may puree soup in a food processor at this point if you prefer a smoother soup. (Allow the soup to cool slightly first.)
8. Add ham and simmer, stirring occasionally, for 15 more minutes.
9. Serve with dollop of sour cream and garnish of pea sprouts.

Gazpacho

Is it a soup, a salad, or a juice? Gazpacho, a chilled soup, is a summer favorite that you can adapt in so many ways so you are able to use whatever is in season or in your refrigerator. Because it is a summer recipe, you will have a variety of wonderful vegetables to choose from when you decide to make this food. Add your sprouts and you have a healthy and vibrant-tasting treat. This recipe is a good starting point for your creative experiments.

This yields eight servings.

Ingredients

1 peeled and diced cucumber

2 cups diced red or green bell pepper

2 cups diced tomato

1 small diced red onion

4 cups cold tomato juice

1 cup radish sprouts

½ cup arugula sprouts

½ of a lemon, juiced

1 lime, juiced

¼ cup red wine vinegar

3 Tbsp. extra virgin olive oil

1 crushed garlic clove

1 tsp. honey

1 tsp. dried tarragon

1 tsp. dried basil

¼ tsp. ground cumin

Hot pepper sauce (to taste)

Directions

1. Place all ingredients in a blender to the desired consistency. (If you cannot fit all the ingredients in your blender, follow steps 2 through 6.)

2. Chop the vegetables and blend them to a course consistency and then transfer the vegetables to a large bowl.

3. Put the remaining ingredients in the blender and blend well.

4. Remove half the liquid from the blender and put it in a bowl.

5. Add half the coarsely chopped vegetable to the remaining liquid in the blender.

6. Blend to desired consistency.

7. Transfer the gazpacho in the blender to a large bowl or container for refrigeration.

8. Place the remaining coarsely chopped vegetable and liquid in the blender and blend to desired consistency.

9. Transfer the gazpacho in the blender to a large bowl or container with the rest of the mixture for refrigeration.

10. Chill for at least two hours.

This recipe is even more flavorful the next day. Try serving this recipe with corn chips.

Southwest Style Sprouted Soup

This recipe yields three to four servings.

Ingredients

1 cup sunflower sprouts

1 cup clover sprouts

Juice of 1 lemon

1 cup buckwheat greens

1 cup sunflower greens

2 cups unchlorinated spring water

1 cup sunflower sprouts (put in bottom of blender)

1 diced ripe avocado

Cayenne pepper (optional)

Directions

1. Place all ingredients except for the avocado and cayenne pepper in a blender.

2. Fill blender 3/4 full of filtered or spring water and blend on high speed until smooth.

3. Add diced avocado to blender and blend for 30 seconds.

Serve in bowls immediately with cayenne pepper.

Beef and Sprouted Barley Stew

This recipe yields six servings.

Ingredients

2 lbs. stew beef

2 Tbsp. olive oil

3 quarts water or beef stock

¾ to 1 cup split peas

¾ to 1 cup sprouted barley

1 bay leaf

1 chopped yellow onion

1 thinly sliced leek

2 thinly sliced carrots

1 thinly sliced turnip

1 thinly sliced parsnip (optional)

2 finely chopped celery stalks

1 crushed garlic clove

½ head chopped cabbage

6 medium peeled and quartered potatoes

Kosher salt (to taste)

12 whole black peppercorns

Directions

1. Soak split peas overnight in cold water.
2. Cut the stew beef into 1½-inch cubes.
3. Put olive oil and beef into a soup pot on medium heat.
4. Brown the stew beef, stirring occasionally.
5. Drain the soaked split peas.
6. Add all the rest of the ingredients except potatoes and cabbage.
7. Increase the heat under the pot to a medium high.
8. Bring the liquid in the pot to a boil, and then reduce the heat to low.
9. Simmer over low heat for two and a half hours.
10. After the soup has been simmering for two and a half hours, stir in the chopped cabbage.
11. In a separate pot, boil or steam the potatoes until tender.
12. When the potatoes are tender, drain them well.
13. Return the potatoes to the hot pan and cover.
14. The stew is done when the split peas are tender (after about three hours).
15. Serve the stew in soup bowl over the cooked potatoes.

Serve with Essene bread (*Chapter 12*).

Chicken and Sprouted Barley Soup

This recipe yields eight servings.

Ingredients

1 cup sprouted barley

1½ cups chicken broth

3 Tbsp. butter

3 Tbsp. flour

8 cups chicken broth

½ cup cream

Salt (to taste)

Fresh ground black pepper (to taste)

Directions

1. Place 1½ cups of chicken broth and 1 cup of sprouted barley in a soup pot.
2. Bring chicken broth to a low boil over medium-high heat.
3. Reduce heat to low.
4. Simmer barley and chicken broth for about 30 minutes.
5. In a separate saucepan, melt butter over medium heat.
6. Use a whisk to stir flour into melted butter to make roux. (Roux is a mixture of a fat such as butter and flour and is used as a thickener.)
7. Pour 8 cups of chicken broth (not the chicken broth with barley) into roux. Use a whisk to incorporate chicken broth with roux.
8. Simmer over medium heat for 30 minutes.
9. Add cream and sprouted barley mixture to soup.
10. Stir well.
11. Season with salt and pepper to taste and serve hot.

Sprouted Barley Vegetable Soup

This recipe yields eight servings.

Ingredients

4 to 5 medium carrots, diced into 1-inch cubes

4 to 5 medium zucchini, diced into 1-inch cubes

3 to 4 onions, diced into 1/2-inch chunks

1 cup white wine

1½ quarts chicken stock or broth

2 cups sprouted barley

2 Tbsp. oregano

2 Tbsp. rosemary

4 Tbsp. olive oil

Salt and pepper to taste

Directions

1. Preheat the oven to 450 degrees.
2. Combine 2 Tbsp. of the olive oil with the salt and pepper. Toss this mixture with the diced zucchini and carrots.
3. Place the vegetables on a sheet pan and roast in the oven for 15 minutes, or until brown.
4. Remove the roasted vegetables from the oven and set aside.
5. Put 2 Tbsp. olive oil and diced onion into a medium soup pot.
6. Cook the onions until golden brown.
7. Add the white wine to the soup pot.
8. Cook until ¾ of the liquid evaporates.
9. Add the roasted vegetables, sprouted barley, herbs, and chicken stock to the pot and allow the soup to simmer for 45 minutes.
10. Season with salt and pepper to taste.

Vegetable Bean Sprouted Soup

This is a very old world recipe that makes a tasty vegetable soup from scratch, starting with homemade vegetable broth.

This yields ten to 12 servings.

Vegetable Broth

Ingredients

1 large bunch of celery with leaves

4 to 6 red onions cut into quarters

4 to 6 large carrots cut into 1-inch pieces

4 cored tomatoes

6 green bell pepper cut into 1-inch pieces

2 cubed turnips

2 Tbsp. olive oil

3 cloves garlic

3 whole cloves

1 bay leaf

8 whole black peppercorns

Directions

1. Preheat oven to 450 degrees.
2. Cut the leaves off the celery ribs and set aside. You will be using the leaves later in the recipe.
3. Put the onions, carrots, tomatoes, bell peppers, and turnips in a large mixing bowl.
4. Add the olive oil to the vegetables.
5. Toss onions, carrots, celery ribs, tomatoes, bell peppers, and turnips with olive oil.

6. Place vegetables in a roasting pan and put them in the oven to roast.
7. Stir the vegetables every ten minutes.
8. Roast for about an hour or until all the vegetables have browned and the onions start to caramelize.
9. Put the browned vegetables, celery leaves, garlic, cloves, bay leaf, peppercorns, parsley, and water into a large stock pot.
10. Bring the water to a full boil over a medium-high heat.
11. Reduce heat to simmer.
12. Allow to simmer uncovered for four to six hours until liquid is reduced by half.
13. Remove from heat and allow the broth to cool for two hours.
14. Pour the broth through a sieve, catching the broth in a pot. The liquid caught in the pot is the vegetable broth you will use.

For the soup

Ingredients

2 quarts vegetable broth (This should just about what you have from the recipe above. If you find yourself a little short, you can add water.)

¼ tsp. fresh ground black pepper

⅛ tsp. kosher salt

1½-inch piece of peeled and finely grated ginger root

2 bay leaves

6 large crushed cloves garlic

2 thinly sliced stalks celery with chopped leaves

½ chopped yellow onion

1 cup mung bean sprouts

1 cup sprouted barley

1 large chopped red bell pepper

3 large peeled and thinly sliced carrots

1 thinly sliced leek

3 chopped Portobello mushrooms

3 chopped scallions

Directions

1. Put all ingredients into a large soup pot over medium-high heat.
2. Bring soup to a boil.
3. Reduce heat to a simmer.
4. Simmer gently for about two hours.
5. Stir occasionally, adding water as needed.

Serve with a dollop of sour cream and any of the sprouted breads or crackers in this book.

Sesame Noodle Soup

This recipe yields four to six servings.

Ingredients

½ pound rice noodles

4 cups chicken stock

1 Tbsp. sesame oil

2 Tbsp. soy sauce

3 Tbsp. sesame seed sprouts

1 Tbsp. fresh ginger, grated

2 minced jalapeños

1 cup sprouted mung beans

1 Tbsp. scallions

1 Tbsp. diced cooked chicken

Directions

1. Cook rice noodles in boiling water according to package directions.
2. Drain rice noodles.
3. Put chicken stock in a medium soup pot.
4. Heat chicken stock over medium-high heat just to a boil.
5. Combine 1 cup chicken stock with sesame oil, soy sauce, sesame seed sprouts, grated fresh ginger, and minced jalapeños.
6. Put drained rice noodles in a large bowl.
7. Add stock and sesame mixture to the rice noodles
8. Put servings of rice noodle mixture in soup bowls.
9. Top rice noodles with sliced scallions, sprouted mung beans, and diced cooked chicken.
10. Ladle additional chicken stock into bowls.

Serve hot.

Sweet Potato Soup with Ginger Shrimp

This recipe yields eight servings.

Ingredients

6 small sweet potatoes, peeled and diced

2 cups unsweetened coconut milk

6 cups chicken broth

3 Tbsp. minced ginger

3 Tbsp. lemon juice

2 Tbsp. peanut oil

1 tsp. coarse kosher salt

1½ pounds medium shrimp, peeled and deveined

4 firm bananas

1 cup unsweetened toasted coconut flakes

1 cup finely chopped soaked almonds

½ cup chopped cilantro

Directions

1. Place peeled and diced sweet potatoes into a large saucepan and add coconut milk and chicken broth to potatoes.
2. Cook sweet potatoes over a medium heat for 15 to 20 minutes until soft.
3. Remove saucepan from heat and allow to cool slightly.
4. Transfer sweet potato, coconut milk, and chicken broth mixture to a blender and puree mixture until smooth.
5. Set sweet potato, coconut milk, and chicken broth mixture aside.
6. Combine minced ginger, lemon juice, peanut oil, and coarse kosher salt in a shallow dish and add shrimp to this mixture.
7. Marinate shrimp in liquid mixture for one hour.
8. Remove shrimp from marinade and sauté shrimp in 1 Tbsp. peanut oil over medium-high heat for three to four minutes until shrimp turns pink.
9. Set shrimp aside.
10. Slice bananas.
11. Sauté bananas in oil over medium-high heat until brown on both sides.
12. Arrange shrimp, bananas, toasted coconut flakes, finely chopped soaked almonds, and cilantro in separate bowls.
13. Place sweet potato, coconut milk, and chicken broth in a large saucepan and reheat just to boiling.
14. Ladle sweet potato, coconut milk, and chicken broth mixture into individual serving bowls.

Serve hot with condiments of shrimp, bananas, toasted coconut flakes, finely chopped soaked almonds, cilantro, and Tabasco.

Curried Mung Sprout Soup

This recipe yields six servings.

Ingredients

4 cups water

1 cup mung bean sprouts

1 Tbsp. rice flour

1 cup buttermilk (You may also use plain yogurt.)

Salt (to taste)

1 tsp. white sugar

1 sprig fresh curry leaves

1 Tbsp. vegetable oil

1 tsp. fresh ground black pepper

1 tsp. ground cumin

1 tsp. chopped fresh cilantro

Directions

1. Pour water into a medium saucepan and bring to a boil.
2. Add bean sprouts to boiling water and cook for three to four minutes.
3. Strain the mung bean sprouts, keeping the water you cooked them in, and set the sprouts aside.
4. Place the water you cooked the mung bean sprouts in the saucepan.
5. Use a whisk to mix rice flour and buttermilk into the mung bean sprout stock.
6. Add sugar and curry leaf to the stock.
7. Season stock with salt to taste.

8. In a separate pan, heat vegetable oil just until it smokes.

9. Add pepper and cumin to pan and sauté for about 30 seconds.

10. Pour pepper and cumin mixture over the soup and bring to a boil.

11. Place 2 Tbsp. mung bean sprouts in a soup bowl.

12. Spoon hot soup over sprouts.

13. Garnish soup with chopped cilantro and serve hot.

Sprouted Soybean Soup

This recipe yields six to eight servings.

Ingredients

1 Tbsp. sesame oil

2 Tbsp. soy sauce

2 crushed cloves garlic

1 scallion

3 cups soybean sprouts

6 cups vegetable broth (see vegetable broth recipe in this chapter)

1 tsp. salt

Bunch of chives (optional garnish)

1 Tbsp. cayenne pepper (optional)

Directions

1. Sauté garlic and scallion in soy sauce and sesame oil in a medium-sized pot over medium heat for two to three minutes.

2. Add vegetable and bean sprouts to pot.

3. Bring soup to a boil over medium-high heat.

4. Reduce to low heat and simmer for 30 minutes.

5. After 25 minutes of simmering, add the cayenne pepper (five minutes before turning off the heat)

6. Add chives just before serving.

Sprouted Lentil Soup —————————————

This recipe yields four to six servings.

Ingredients

2 Tbsp. peanut oil

1 minced onion

2 crushed cloves garlic

1 tsp. celery seeds

1 tsp. dried thyme

¼ tsp. dried tarragon

4 Tbsp. tomato paste

4 cups vegetable broth (see vegetable broth recipe in this chapter)

2 sliced medium carrots

1 cup sprouted amaranth

3 cups sprouted lentils

Directions

1. Heat the peanut oil in a sauté pan until it just begins to smoke.
2. Add and sauté the onion and garlic for one minute.
3. Add the celery seeds, thyme, and tarragon to sautéed onion and garlic and sauté for one minute.
4. Transfer onion, garlic, and spice mixture to a medium soup pot.
5. Add tomato paste, vegetable broth, and carrots to soup pot and bring to a boil.
6. Add sprouted amaranth and sprouted lentils to soup and lower heat.
7. Simmer soup for 15 minutes before serving.

Peanut Sprout Soup

This recipe yields six servings.

Ingredients

1 cup smooth peanut butter (Use the kind that is made with only peanuts and a little or no salt.)

2 Tbsp. peanut oil

½ tsp. cayenne pepper

1 Tbsp. fresh grated ginger

1 finely chopped white onion

1 crushed clove garlic

4 cups vegetable stock

1 Tbsp. tomato paste

Hot pepper sauce, such as Tabasco (to taste)

Salt (to taste)

Sugar (to taste)

1½ cups fresh peanut sprouts

Directions

1. Heat the peanut oil in a saucepan.
2. Add the chopped onions and sauté until soft.
3. Add garlic and allow it to lightly brown.
4. Add the vegetable stock and the peanut butter and use a whisk to combine.
5. Add tomato paste and spices, stirring the mixture frequently.
6. Allow soup to simmer.
7. Season to taste with salt, hot pepper sauce, and sugar.
8. Add 1½ cups fresh peanut sprouts just before serving. Do not cook with the peanut sprouts as they will become quite rubbery.

Serve in bowls with rice.

Soups can be made as a light fare enjoyed with other dishes, or as stand-alone hearty main courses. They are also very forgiving and can be made with many substitutions. Have fun and experiment with any of the above soups.

If you have a little more room after enjoying your soup, try one of the sandwich recipes in the next chapter.

CASE STUDY: CHRIS LINCOLN

Chris Lincoln
New Minglewood Farm
www.newminglewoodfarm.com

Chris Lincoln of New Minglewood Farm has been growing a variety of sprouts on a small commercial scale to sell at a local farmer's market for 11 years. New Minglewood Farm is a small diversified vegetable farm.

"Sprouts are a crop we can produce consistently every week of our market season," Lincoln said. "They are a great healthy product, easy to grow (regardless of the weather), and no one else at our market sells them."

"The old saying is true – you are what you eat. So if you are alive, shouldn't you be eating 'living food?' Sprouts are the ultimate living food. Most fruits and vegetables start to decrease in vitamin content as soon as you pick them. Sprouts, however, are still alive when you eat them and are at their peak of nutritional value. In fact, through a metabolic process in the seed when it is sprouted, the nutritional value greatly increases from that of an unsprouted seed."

"The vitamin C in sprouted peas increases eightfold in four days (compared to dry peas). Likewise, the vitamin B-complex in wheat increases by six times and vitamin E by three times just in four days of sprouting. There are also many minerals and enzymes in sprouts in a form that the body can use immediately."

"In addition to high nutrition, broccoli sprouts also have a high concentration of glucoraphanin. Scientific studies have discovered that people with diets high in this chemical have a reduced risk of stomach cancer and also a lower risk of developing ulcers. There may also be a link to lower risk for colon, breast, and liver cancers. A single ounce of broccoli sprouts has as much glucoraphanin as a pound and a quarter of cooked broccoli." "Eating broccoli sprouts or any of our other 'green' sprouts are an excellent way to boost vitamins in your diet – from a natural sourcerather than a pill. They are also easy to use – top off a fresh mixed salad or use instead of lettuce on your favorite sandwich." "Bean sprouts are also high in vitamins, but have the added advantage of being a good source of protein. One cup of raw mung bean sprouts has 4 grams of protein. They can be used fresh like green sprouts or lightly cooked. We like to use them with stir-fried vegetables or toss them in with pasta dishes."

"The easiest for us to sprout are beans. We do a mix of mung, lentil, and adzuki that only take about three days. Alfalfa tends to rot very easily, so we switched to clover, which is similar, but a lot easier to grow. I would love to know how to grow a healthy arugula sprout, but have had no success."

"There are many seeds we have not tried to sprout. We stick mostly with the standard stuff: clover, broccoli, radish, mustard, beans. We grow sunflower shoots on soil trays."

Lincoln said his farm's seeds are certified organic so by law he must sell organic seeds. Perhaps even more important in his mind is the quality of the seeds you consume. He said, "Find a company that sells clean seed with good germination. If it's also organic, all the better."

He said one of the ways he enjoys bean sprouts is to use them to make veggie burgers. He said you can make them ahead of time and freeze them later to make a quick meal. The following is one recipe he has used. He said, "The variations are endless, so be creative!"

Bean Sprout Veggie Burgers

These veggie burgers are a welcome summer lunch or dinner for meat-eaters and vegetarians alike. They are high in protein, very low in fat, and taste great. They can be made ahead of time and then frozen so they are on hand for quick suppers. This recipe will make ten to 12 burgers.

Ingredients

2 Tbsp. olive oil 2 small onions, chopped (approx. 1 cup)

1 cup celery, chopped (or green peppers, mushrooms, or grated carrot, depending on your tastes or what you have in the refrigerator or garden)

1 to 2 cloves of garlic, minced (use to taste)

1 lb. New Minglewood Bean Spout mix (4 cups)

2 Tbsp. tamari or soy sauce

¼ cup ketchup

1 egg

1½ cups bread crumbs

Black pepper, to taste

Chili version: 1½ Tbsp. chili powder

Curry version: 1½ Tbsp. curry powder

Italian version: 2 tsp. oregano, 2 tsp. basil

Directions

1. Preheat oven to 350 degrees.
2. Sauté onions, garlic, and celery (or other vegetables) in oil until onions are translucent. Place bean sprouts, tamari (or soy sauce), ketchup, and fried vegetables in food processor.
3. Process until bean sprouts are well chopped.
4. Add egg and spices to processed bean sprouts in a medium bowl.
5. Stir breadcrumbs into bean sprout and egg mixture.
6. Allow to sit for ten minutes.
7. Lightly grease a cookie sheet.
8. Form "burgers" by hand with approximately □ cup of bean mixture.
9. Place "burgers" on cookie sheet.
10. Bake 30 minutes at 350 degrees.

To freeze the burgers, place plastic-wrap or waxed paper between layers in a freezer container before freezing. Defrost and warm in oven or lightly fry.

Chapter 9

Sandwiches

S andwiches are easy, healthy treats that you can make as snacks or as full meals. As always, do not be afraid to mix, match, and experiment with the suggested ingredients.

Sprout and Salad Sandwiches

This recipe yields four to six servings.

Yogurt Cucumber Dressing

Ingredients

1 cup plain fat-free yogurt

½ cup diced seedless cucumber

¼ cup minced red onion

1 tsp. fresh lemon juice

Directions

1. Mix all ingredients in a small bowl.
2. Cover and chill.

Sprout Salad Sandwich

Ingredients

4 medium-pocket breads (pita)

1 cucumber, thinly sliced

1 medium tomato, sliced

½ cup broccoli sprouts

½ cup radish sprouts

½ cup lentil sprouts

½ cup pea sprouts

½ cup yogurt cucumber dressing

Directions for sandwich

1.   Cut pita in half across its diameter.
2.   Spread yogurt cucumber dressing inside each of the halved pitas.
3.   Arrange layers of vegetables on both sides.
4.   Stuff the middle with mixed sprouts.

Healthy Grilled Cheese

Everyone loves a good grilled cheese sandwich, and this has to be about the best. Here is an extremely healthy take on an old favorite. This will make you one delicious grilled cheese sandwich.

Ingredients

2 slices of wheat berry sunflower bread or sprouted oatmeal bread (*You will learn how to make these in Chapter 12.*)

2 sharp cheddar cheese slices (or whatever good melting cheese you prefer)

2 Tbsp. butter

2 thin tomato slices

2 Tbsp. radish sprouts

2 Tbsp. buckwheat sprouts

2 Tbsp. sunflower seed sprouts

Directions

1. Place a slice of cheese on a single bread slice.
2. Place second bread slice on top of cheese.
3. Lightly butter the top of the sandwich.
4. Melt remaining butter in a skillet over medium-low heat.
5. Place sandwich, butter side up, in skillet.
6. Cover and cook for about two minutes.
7. Remove cover.
8. Use a spatula to check the bottom of the sandwich to see if it is golden brown.
9. If sandwich is golden brown, flip it butter side down. (If it is not golden brown, return it to pan and cook covered for another minute or two.)
10. Cover the skillet and cook the sandwich butter side down for one or two minutes.
11. Uncover the skillet (Cheese should be melted at this point).
12. Lift with spatula and check bottom for golden brown color.
13. When both sides are cooked to a golden brown, remove sandwich from skillet.
14. Place sandwich on a plate.
15. Carefully lift top piece of bread.
16. Place two thin tomato slices, 2 Tbsp. radish sprouts, 2 Tbsp. buckwheat sprouts, and 2 Tbsp. sunflower seed sprouts on cheese.
17. Place bread back on top of sprout sandwich.
18. Lightly salt top of sandwich (optional).

Slice diagonally and serve warm.

Avocado Sprout Sandwich

This recipe yields one sandwich.

Ingredients

2 slices of wheat berry sunflower bread or sprouted oatmeal bread (*see Chapter 12*)

1 ripe avocado

2 thin tomato slices

1 thinly sliced red onion

Mayonnaise (to taste)

Salt (to taste)

Fresh ground black pepper (to taste)

Crushed red pepper flakes (to taste)

2 Tbsp. radish sprouts

2 Tbsp. buckwheat sprouts

2 Tbsp. sunflower seed sprouts

Directions

1. Slice the avocado in half and peel the outside off the flesh.
2. Remove the avocado pit.
3. Lay the avocado half down on the flat side and slice it thinly lengthwise.
4. Set aside.
5. Spread a thin layer of mayonnaise to cover each slice of bread.
6. Lightly sprinkle salt and pepper over both mayonnaise-covered bread slices.
7. Sprinkle crushed red pepper flakes over a single bread slice.
8. Add a thin layer of avocado slices, tomato slices, onion slices, and the sprouts to the bread slice.
9. Cover with the other mayonnaise-covered bread slice.

Slice diagonally and serve.

Mock Chicken Salad Sandwich

This recipe yields four servings.

Ingredients

1 cup soaked almonds

1 cup sprouted sunflower seeds

¼ cup sprouted sesame seeds

2 crushed garlic cloves

2 Tbsp. lemon juice

3 to 4 Tbsp. mayonnaise

½ cup finely chopped celery

½ cup finely chopped red onion

½ cup finely chopped parsley

Directions

1. Put the soaked almonds, sprouted sunflower seeds, sprouted sesame seeds, crushed garlic, lemon juice, and mayonnaise in the bowl of a food processor.
2. Process the ingredients until they are combined, though not entirely smooth.
3. Transfer processed mixture to a mixing bowl.
4. Add remaining ingredients to processed nut/sprout mixture and mix well.
5. Serve on sprouted crackers or bread topped with alfalfa sprouts.

Sprout and Soy Veggie Burgers

This yields eight servings.

Ingredients

1 cup soy beans

1 cup adzuki sprouts

1 cup lentil sprouts

½ cup mung bean sprouts

½ cup chick pea sprouts

1¼ tsp. salt

½ tsp. pepper

2 Tbsp. canola oil

½ cup flour

¼ cup milk

2 eggs, beaten

3 finely chopped scallions

2 crushed cloves garlic

1 Tbsp. dried thyme

1 Tbsp. dried marjoram

Directions

1. The night before, put the soy beans in a pot and cover them with water. Allow the beans to soak overnight.

2. The next day, drain the soy beans and cover them with fresh water.

3. Put the pot of soy beans over medium heat.

4. When the water comes to a boil, turn the heat to low and allow the soy beans to cook on a low heat for two and a half hours, or until the soy beans are soft. (Be sure that the soy beans are always covered by water.)

5. After the soy beans have cooked, drain them in a colander.

6. Put the adzuki sprouts, lentil sprouts, mung bean sprouts, and chick pea sprouts in a food processor.

7. Grind the sprouts in a food processor until they are roughly chopped.

8. Transfer the chopped sprouts to a large mixing bowl.

9. Put the cooked soy beans in the food processor and process until they form a thick, smooth paste.

10. Add the soy bean paste to the large mixing bowl with the chopped sprouts.

11. Add all the other ingredients to the bowl and mix well.

12. Form the mixture into ¼-inch patties.

13. Heat skillet over medium-high heat for one minute.

14. Add oil and heat until almost smoking (about one minute).

15. Place patties in pan and brown lightly on each side.

Serve on whole wheat burger buns with your choice of condiments.

Veggie Nut Burgers

This yields eight to ten servings.

Ingredients

1 cup soaked almonds

1 cup sunflower seeds soaked in water for six to eight hours and rinsed

1 beet

1 red bell pepper

1 red onion

1 zucchini

2 finely grated carrots

2 ribs finely chopped celery

¼ cup finely chopped fresh basil

¼ cup finely chopped fresh parsley

2 tsp. olive oil

2 Tbsp. lemon juice

Directions

1. Place soaked almonds in a bowl and cover them with boiling water.
2. Allow the almonds sit in hot water for only one minute.
3. Drain almonds and then rinse then under cold water.
4. Allow almonds to drain.
5. Place almonds, sunflower seeds, beet, red bell pepper, onion, and zucchini in the bowl of a food processor and process for about 30 seconds.
6. Transfer nut mixture to a large mixing bowl.
7. Add remaining ingredients to nut mixture.
8. Form mixture into round burgers about ¾-inch thick.
9. Heat 2 Tbsp. olive oil in a large skillet over medium heat.
10. Cook burgers about three minutes each side until heated through.

Serve on buns topped with sprouts, tomato, and avocado.

Veggie Burger and Sprouts

Falafel and Sprout Sandwich ————————•

The chickpeas in this recipe are not sprouted, but soaked and cooked. The nutty crispness of the alfalfa sprouts is a perfect complement to the smoothness of the mashed chickpeas.

This recipe yields eight servings.

Ingredients

4 cups cooked chickpeas (garbanzo beans)

3 cloves crushed garlic

2 beaten eggs

3 Tbsp. tahini

3 Tbsp. unbleached white flour

½ cup finely chopped scallions

½ tsp. ground cumin

½ tsp. turmeric

¼ tsp. cayenne pepper

4 pieces of pita bread

1 thinly sliced tomato

1 cup yogurt cucumber dressing (See the sprout salad sandwich recipe
   earlier in this chapter.)

2 loose cups of alfalfa sprouts

Directions

1. Soak chickpeas in water in a saucepan overnight.

2. The next day, drain chickpeas and cover with fresh water.

3. Put the saucepan on the stove over a medium-high heat and bring the water to a boil.

4. Allow water to boil over medium-high heat for five minutes.

5. Turn heat to low.

6. Allow chickpeas to simmer on low for one hour and 15 minutes.

7. Remove chickpeas from heat and drain in a colander.

8. Allow chickpeas to cool for about 20 minutes.

9. Place chickpeas, crushed garlic, eggs, tahini, flour, scallions, cumin, turmeric, and cayenne pepper into a food processor.

10. Process to a rough consistency.

11. Flour your fingers and form 1-inch balls (about the size of a walnut) out of the chickpea batter.

12. Lightly dust each ball with flour.

13. In a deep skillet, heat a 2-inch deep pool of canola oil to 360 to 375 degrees. (If you do not have an instant-read thermometer, you will know that the oil is ready by putting a chopstick or wooden spoon into the oil. If bubbles form around it, the oil is hot enough.)

14. Fry the chickpea ball (falafel) in the oil until it is completely golden brown.

15. Transfer the falafel to a dish lined with paper towel.

16. Place two warm falafels in a halved pit pocket.

17. Top with sliced tomato, yogurt cucumber dressing, and alfalfa sprouts.

When you think about the sandwiches listed in this chapter, also consider the bread recipes included in Chapter 12. The sprouted breads combined with sprouted fillings make for a satisfying and healthy meal.

Chapter 10

Stir-Fry

Stir-frying is a classic way to serve many different kinds of sprouts. The traditional sprouts used in stir-fry dishes are bean sprouts, especially soy beans and mung beans. Included here are some recipes that will be new to you, as well as several popular favorites.

Soybean Sprouts in Ginger

This is a very easy recipe that has a great nutty and gingery flavor. If you are wild about ginger, feel free to use more than the amount the recipe states. This dish is a great side dish for fish (especially salmon) or roasted poultry.

This recipe yields four servings.

Ingredients
1 Tbsp. peanut oil
1 Tbsp. finely grated fresh ginger root
4 cups soybean sprouts (*sprouted as per directions in Chapter 4*)
¼ cup sprouted sesame seeds
Soy sauce (to taste)

Sesame oil (to taste)

Directions

1. Pour the peanut oil into a wok, moving the wok around to coat both the bottom and the sides. (You can do this by swirling peanut oil around in the wok as it heats.)
2. Heat the peanut oil over a medium-high heat.
3. Add half of the grated ginger and stir it around for about a minute.
4. Add the soybean sprouts.
5. Stir the soybean sprouts to coat them with the oil and ginger.
6. Allow the soybean sprouts to cook for about five minutes, stirring occasionally.
7. After five minutes, add the rest of the ginger and soy sauce to taste.
8. Allow the soybean sprouts to cook for about five minutes, stirring occasionally.
9. Add sesame oil to taste.

Serve hot over brown rice.

Pad Thai

Here is a classic Thai recipe. You can include shrimp as mentioned in this recipe, or you can make a vegetarian version by replacing the shrimp and chicken stock with cashews and vegetable stock, respectively.

This recipe yields two servings.

Ingredients

8 oz. Thai rice noodles

2 to 3 Tbsp. peanut oil

1 small, finely chopped red onion

4 cloves minced garlic

2-inch section ginger root, peeled and thinly sliced

1 to 2 fresh red chilies, finely sliced

1 to 2 cups raw or cooked shrimp, shells removed

3 Tbsp. chicken stock

1 egg

2 to 3 cups mung bean sprouts

¼ tsp. fresh ground black pepper

3 finely chopped scallions

½ cup fresh cilantro

½ cup chopped dry roasted peanuts

1 lime sliced into wedges

2 thin cabbage wedges

Pad Thai Sauce Ingredients

½ cup brown sugar

½ cup distilled white vinegar

¼ cup soy sauce

2 Tbsp. tamarind pulp (available at Asian/Indian food stores)

½ to 1 tsp. dried crushed chili pepper (to taste)

Directions

1. Fill a large pot with water and bring to a boil.
2. Remove pot from heat.
3. Put the rice noodles in the hot water to soak.
4. Allow the noodles to soak in the hot water until soft. (The noodle should be al dente — soft but still slightly firm.)
5. Drain the noodles in a colander.
6. Rinse the noodles thoroughly with cold water.
7. Set the noodles aside.

8. Place the sauce ingredients (brown sugar, white vinegar, soy sauce, tamarind pulp, and crushed chili peppers) in a small sauce pan.

9. Heat the ingredients over a medium heat, stirring frequently.

10. Heat the sauce ingredients until hot and blended well.

11. Set sauce aside.

12. Heat a wok over medium-high heat.

13. Add 2 Tbsp. peanut oil to wok.

14. Immediately add the red onion, garlic, ginger root, and chili and stir-fry for one minute.

15. Add the shrimp and the chicken stock.

16. Stir-fry two to three minutes, or until shrimp are pink and plump. (If using cooked shrimp, only stir-fry for one minute.)

17. Make a well in the center of the wok by moving all ingredients away from the center of the wok.

18. Add 1 Tbsp. peanut oil to the well in the center of the wok.

19. Break the egg into the well.

20. Stir-fry the egg (30 seconds to one minute) to scramble in the well.

21. Add the drained noodles, mung bean sprouts, and the Pad Thai sauce to cover the ingredients in the wok.

22. Gently toss all ingredients in the wok together and stir-fry for four to six minutes.

23. Remove from heat and taste.

24. Add additional chili or soy sauce to suit your taste.

Serve on plates and top with scallion, cilantro, and peanuts, and garnish with lime wedges and cabbage wedges. You can squeeze lime over this dish before serving with extra hot pepper sauce.

Egg Foo Yong

Egg foo yong is an American take on an Asian dish known as fu yong eggs. Quite simply, egg foo yong is a wonderful omelet dish that originated in Shanghai. Egg foo yong is tasty and easy to make.

This recipe yields four servings.

Ingredients

4 Tbsp. peanut oil

½ cup chopped scallion

1 chopped red bell pepper

1 chopped green bell pepper

1 to 2 cups raw or cooked shrimp, shells removed

2 cups mung bean sprouts

6 eggs

½ tsp. soy sauce

⅛ tsp. pepper

Directions

1. Heat a wok over medium-high heat.
2. Add 2 Tbsp. peanut oil to wok.
3. Immediately add the scallion and bell peppers.
4. Stir-fry the scallion and bell peppers for one minute.
5. Add the shrimp and stir-fry for two or three minutes, or until shrimp are pink and plump. (If using cooked shrimp, only stir-fry one minute.)
6. Remove vegetables and shrimp from wok and set aside.
7. Beat eggs with a whisk for one minute in a large bowl. 8. Add the mung bean sprouts, shrimp, sautéed vegetables, and soy sauce to the eggs.

8. Add the mung bean sprouts, shrimp, sautéed vegetables, and soy sauce to the eggs.

9. Heat ½ tsp. of peanut oil on high heat for two minutes in a large skillet.

10. Reduce heat to medium.

11. Use a ladle to transfer ½ cup egg mixture onto hot skillet.

12. Cook egg mixture until set and browned around edges.

13. Flip the egg mixture and brown on other side.

14. After each egg patty is cooked, transfer it to a warm plate.

Serve on a bed of rice with fresh raw vegetables.

Chop Suey

Loosely translated, chop suey means "mixed pieces" in Cantonese. Chop suey is a dish that you can endlessly experiment with as you mix and match a variety of meats, vegetables, and sauce ingredients. Try it with rice or noodles of different sorts while you are experimenting.

This recipe yields four servings.

Ingredients

1½ lb. beef cubes or 1 lb. beef and ½ lb. shredded pork

½ cup chopped yellow onion

1 cup chopped celery

2 Tbsp. brown sugar

2 Tbsp. molasses

4 Tbsp. soy sauce

2 cups mung bean sprouts

1 cup thinly sliced water chestnuts

½ cup chopped scallions

1 sliced green bell pepper

½ cup chopped bamboo shoots

1 cup sliced mushrooms

1 cup water

Chow mein noodles

Directions

1. Heat a wok over medium-high heat.
2. Add meat to heated wok and brown the meat.
3. Add onion and celery to meat as it browns.
4. Add sugar, molasses, and soy sauce. Stir mixture to combine and dissolve sugar.
5. Cover and cook five minutes.
6. Add bean sprouts, water chestnuts, scallions, green bell pepper, bamboo shoots, mushrooms, and water.
7. Stir occasionally. Add more water if needed.
8. Reduce heat to low and cook over low heat for one hour.
9. Serve on top of chow mein noodles or rice.

Bustin' with Brassica

Brassica is the family of vegetables that broccoli, Brussels sprouts, and cabbage belong to. One of the most misunderstood members of this family is kale. You will often find kale used as an adornment on salad bars, placed there not for consumption, but for decoration. Combined with its brassica brother broccoli sprouts in this recipe, you would be hard-pressed to eat much healthier than this.

This recipe yields to four servings.

Ingredients

1 large bunch of kale

2 Tbsp. olive oil

1 Tbsp. butter

2 large cloves of minced garlic

1 medium chopped onion

1 Tbsp. ginger root (The ginger root can be thinly sliced, minced, or grated.)

1 cup of broccoli sprouts

1 cup radish sprouts

½ cup sesame seed sprouts

1 lime, juiced

Fresh ground black pepper (to taste)

Directions

1. Steam kale until slightly wilted, or limp (about four minutes).
2. In a wok or large skillet, heat olive oil and butter over a medium-high heat.
3. Add garlic, onion, and ginger to the wok.
4. Stir garlic, onion, and ginger in oil until the onion is soft.
5. Add kale to garlic, onion, and ginger.
6. Cover wok/skillet and reduce heat to low.
7. Cook until kale is tender (about ten minutes).
8. Add lime juice to kale.
9. Add radish sprouts, broccoli sprouts, and sesame sprouts just prior to serving.
10. Add fresh ground black pepper to taste.

Broccoli Bok Choy Stir-Fry with Mung Bean Sprouts

This recipe yields to four servings.

Ingredients

2 Tbsp. peanut oil

1 tsp. sesame oil

1 red bell pepper cut into small strips

1 green bell pepper cut into small strips

1 thinly sliced medium onion

1 Tbsp. freshly grated ginger root

1 cup broccoli florets

1 cup mung bean sprouts

2 cloves garlic, minced

½ tsp. salt (to taste)

¼ tsp. red pepper flakes (to taste)

1 lb. coarsely chopped bok choy (Bok choy is a member of the mustard family with a head of green leaves and a long white stem.)

2 Tbsp. lemon juice

1 Tbsp. soy sauce

1½ tsp. honey

Directions

1. Heat peanut oil in a large skillet or wok over medium-high heat.
2. Add red bell pepper, green bell pepper, onion, ginger, garlic, salt, and red pepper flakes to large skillet or wok.
3. Stir-fry for two minutes.
4. Add in broccoli and bok choy and stir-fry for one to two minutes.
5. Add mung bean sprouts, lemon juice, soy sauce, and honey.
6. Stir-fry for three minutes or until crisp-tender.

Serve over rice or noodles.

Any of the recipes listed above can easily be considered a main dish or a substantial side dish. For more great main and side dish recipes, the following chapter with show you many ways that you can incorporate sprouts into classic recipes such as meatloaf. It will also offer some new ways to add the healthy benefits of sprouts to your breakfast, lunch, and/or dinner.

Chapter 11

Main Dishes and Side Dishes

You will see that you can do amazing things with sprouts in your main dish recipes. You can use various kinds of sprouts in place of or as a complement to meat. Sprouts can give main dishes a huge protein lift and add to the flavor and texture of your favorite dish. Many of the recipes here, you will find, are favorite dishes (such as meatloaf and lasagna) that sprouts can enhance.

Sprouted Barley Meatloaf

While this is not a vegetarian dish, it is a good mixture of meat and sprouts. This recipe yields four to six servings.

Ingredients

1 tsp. extra virgin olive oil

1 cup chopped white onion

½ cup grated carrots

½ cup pearled barley (This is barley that has the outer bran layer removed.)

1¼ cups beef or chicken stock (depending on what kind of meat you choose to use)

1½ lbs. ground beef or turkey

½ cup sprouted barley

1 Tbsp. brown sugar

2 large eggs

1 tsp. dried thyme

1 tsp. dried marjoram

½ tsp. salt

½ tsp. pepper

For topping

3 Tbsp. tomato sauce

1 Tbsp. stone-ground horseradish mustard

1 Tbsp. brown sugar

Directions

1. Heat the oil in a large sauté pan until just before it begins to smoke.
2. Add the onions and carrots to the pan and sauté the vegetables until they are soft.
3. Add pearled barley and stock and bring the mixture to a boil.
4. Cook for 30 minutes.
5. When all the stock is absorbed, transfer the mixture to a colander to drain.
6. Allow mixture to cool completely.
7. Preheat oven to 350 degrees.
8. When the pearled barley is completely cool, put it in a large bowl with the turkey, sprouted barley, brown sugar, eggs, thyme, marjoram, salt, and pepper.
9. Mix the ingredients of the bowl well.
10. Prepare a loaf pan by coating the inside of it with vegetable shortening.

11. Shape the ingredients into a loaf and transfer the loaf into the pan.
12. Bake loaf at 350 degrees for one hour.
13. Mix together the tomato sauce, stone-ground horseradish mustard, and brown sugar in a small bowl.
14. Spread the tomato sauce mixture over the loaf.
15. Return loaf to oven.
16. Bake for 30 minutes more at 350 degrees, or until the inside of the loaf registers 160 degrees on a thermometer.

You can serve this meatloaf with mashed potatoes.

Black Turtle Bean Sprouts with Chorizo and Rice

This recipe yields six servings.

Ingredients
4 Tbsp. olive oil
1½ cups chopped red onion
4 cloves minced garlic
1 diced sweet red pepper
3 cups black turtle bean sprouts
¾ cup water
¼ tsp. cayenne pepper
1 bay leaf
½ tsp. white pepper
1 tsp. salt
¼ lb. chorizo sausage (optional; see recipe that follows)
2 cups brown rice

Directions
1. Heat 2 Tbsp. olive oil in a large pan over medium-high heat.

2. When olive oil is just hot enough to smoke, sauté half of the onion, garlic, bell pepper, salt, cayenne, and white peppers.

3. When onions are soft, add the black turtle bean sprouts along with the bay leaf and water. Mix well.

4. Cover and reduce heat to low.

5. Cook over low heat for 45 minutes or until beans are tender.

6. Cook 2 cups of rice in 4 cups of water with a pinch of salt for 30 to 45 minutes, or until all the water has been soaked up.

Meanwhile — directions for chorizo

Ingredients

6 oz. chiles (guajillos or anchos)

⅔ cup vinegar

5 peeled garlic cloves

2 lbs. ground pork

1 Tbsp. paprika

2 tsp. dried oregano

1 tsp. salt

½ tsp. ground cumin

½ tsp. ground coriander

½ tsp. black pepper

½ tsp. ground allspice

Directions

1. Wipe the chiles clean and remove stems.

2. Cut chiles length-wise and remove seeds.

3. Place chiles in a small bowl and cover with hot water. Allow the chiles to soak for 30 minutes.

4. Drain chiles and place in a blender.

5. Add vinegar and garlic cloves to chiles in blender.

6. Purée until smooth.
7. Set chile mixture aside.
8. Place the pork in a large bowl.
9. Add paprika, oregano, salt, cumin, coriander, pepper, and allspice to pork.
10. Mix pork and spices well.
11. Add the chili sauce to the pork mixture and mix well.

Continue with black turtle bean sprouts

12. Heat the remaining 2 Tbsp. olive oil in another pan.
13. Sauté the chorizo lightly until brown.
14. Serve the chorizo sauté over the beans and rice.

Sprouted Black Bean Burritos with Salsa

This recipe yields 12 servings.

Ingredients for burrito filling
1½ cups sprouted black turtle beans
1½ cups sprouted red lentils

Ingredients for salsa
1 large finely chopped tomato
8 to 10 finely chopped tomatillos
¼ cup freshly chopped cilantro
¼ cup tomato juice
2 Tbsp. finely chopped jalapeno pepper
2 tsp. crushed garlic, minced
1 Tbsp. lime juice

¼ tsp. chili powder

¼ tsp. ground cumin

Salt (to taste)

Fresh ground black pepper (to taste)

1 finely chopped red bell pepper

1 finely chopped green bell pepper

⅓ cup chopped scallions

Ingredients for the burritos

12 large tortillas

4 cups cooked brown rice

Grated Monterey Jack cheese (optional)

Sour cream (optional)

Sprouted guacamole (*see recipe in Chapter 6*)

Directions

1. Combine sprouted black turtle beans and lentils in a bowl.
2. Place the chopped tomato, chopped tomatillos, cilantro, tomato juice, jalapeno peppers, crushed garlic, lime juice, chili powder, ground cumin, salt, and pepper in the bowl of a food processor.
3. Pulse the ingredients in the food processor until they are at a desired consistency.
4. Pour the ingredients of the food processor into a mixing bowl.
5. Add the red bell pepper, green bell pepper, and chopped scallions to the tomato mixture.
6. Heat a skillet over low heat.
7. Place a tortilla on the warmed skillet and heat for about one minute.
8. Flip the tortilla and heat the other side for about one minute.
9. Transfer heated tortilla to a serving plate.

10. Put 3 Tbsp. cooked rice, 3 to 4 Tbsp. sprouted black turtle beans and lentils, 4 Tbsp. salsa, and any of the optional ingredients onto the center of the heated tortilla.
11. Roll the burrito wrapper around the ingredients.
12. Continue steps 7 through 11 until you have made all the burritos you need.

Feijoada (Fay–ZHWA–dah)

This is considered the national dish of Brazil. Feijoada was developed by slaves that made it with the meat cuts their masters did not use. As such, this was originally made with ears, snout, tail, and other discarded meats. Below are two recipes for this hearty dish. The first recipe is one that uses a variety of meat cuts (though it is not necessary to use ears, snouts, or tails) you can find in your local supermarket. The recipe that follows is an excellent vegetarian version. Both recipes can be served over rice as a main dish.

Traditional Feijoada

This recipe yields six to eight servings.

Ingredients

5 cups sprouted and cooked black beans

3 cups water

1 cup sprouted barley

½ lb. sausage cut into 1-inch pieces (A good smoked sausage, such as Polish sausage, works well in this recipe.)

½ lb. beef cut into 1-inch cubes (any cut of beef will do)

½ lb. pork cut into 1-inch cubes (any cut of pork will do)

3 slices of thick sliced bacon cut in 1-inch pieces

1 finely chopped jalapeno pepper

1 finely chopped tomato

3 finely chopped cloves garlic

Salt (to taste)

Pepper (to taste)

Cayenne pepper (to taste)

2 oranges peeled and divided into sections

Directions for cooking sprouted black beans

1. Put 8 cups of water and 2½ cups of sprouted black beans in a large pot.
2. Bring water and beans to a boil.
3. Reduce water to a simmer.
4. Cook sprouted black beans for about ten minutes until soft.
5. Drain beans in a colander.

This will give you about 5 cups of sprouted black beans

Directions for traditional feijoada

1. Put drained sprouted beans with 3 cups of water in large saucepan.
2. Bring water to boil over medium-high heat.
3. Reduce water to simmer.
4. Cover saucepan and cook for about 30 minutes, stirring frequently.
5. Add sausage, beef, and pork to beans.
6. Stir stew well.
7. Cover saucepan and cook over medium heat for about 45 minutes, stirring frequently.
8. If the stew gets a little too thick, add a little hot water to prevent sticking.
9. While the stew is simmering, fry bacon in a small skillet over medium heat until crisp.

10. Add jalapeno, tomato, and garlic to bacon and mix well.
11. Reduce heat to low.
12. Simmer bacon and vegetable mixture for five minutes.
13. Add bacon and vegetables to saucepan with beans and meat mixture.
14. Add salt, pepper, and red pepper to taste and mix well.
15. Remove from heat and serve hot over rice.

Garnish this dish with with orange slices.

Vegetarian Feijoada

This recipe yields six servings.

Ingredients

2 cups chopped red onions
3 crushed garlic cloves
1 cup chopped celery
2 chopped green bell peppers
½ cup water
1 18 oz.-can whole tomatoes
½ cup chopped fresh cilantro
¼ tsp. dried thyme
½ tsp. ground fennel
1 tsp. ground coriander
1 cup sprouted barley
5 cups sprouted and cooked black beans
Salt (to taste)
2 Tbsp. olive oil
1½ pounds collard greens

Directions

1. Put the chopped red onions, crushed garlic cloves, chopped celery, chopped green bell peppers, ½ cup water, and the liquid from the canned tomatoes in a large sauce pan.

2. Crush the canned tomatoes in a colander over the sauce pan, allowing the liquid to drain into the pan.

3. Chop the crushed tomatoes and set them aside.

4. Put the sauce pan with vegetables on a medium-high heat.

5. Bring the vegetables to a boil and cook for about 15 minutes.

6. Lower heat to medium low

7. Add ½ cup chopped fresh cilantro, ¼ tsp. dried thyme, ½ tsp. ground fennel, and 1 tsp. ground coriander to the vegetables in the sauce pan.

8. Add 1 cup sprouted barley and 5 cups sprouted and cooked black beans to the vegetables in the sauce pan.

9. Simmer stew over a low heat for about 20 minutes.

10. While stew is simmering, clean and remove stems from collard greens.

11. Roughly chop collard greens.

12. Heat 2 Tbsp. olive oil in a large skillet or wok.

13. Just as the olive oil starts to smoke, add collard greens to skillet.

14. Stir the collard greens and cover.

15. Remove skillet cover and stir collard greens every three to five minutes until collard greens are tender (about 12 minutes).

Serve collard greens hot with feijoada and white rice.

Sprouted Mung Bean Omelet

This recipe yields two to three servings.

Ingredients

1 cup mung bean sprouts

½ cup diced red bell pepper

¼ cup diced green onion

½ cup sliced button mushrooms

¼ cup finely diced tomato

4 large eggs

¼ cup skim milk

2 tsp. canola oil

Directions

1. Sauté vegetables and bean sprouts in oil for three to five minutes in an omelet pan.
2. Remove vegetables and place on a warm plate or in a warm oven.
3. Whisk together the eggs and milk.
4. Pour egg mixture into the omelet pan.
5. Cook the eggs over a medium heat.
6. Stir the loose egg on the top of the omelet by moving the un-cooked portion of the egg to the side of the pan with a fork.
7. When the egg is nearly entirely set on top, spoon vegetables in center of eggs and fold omelet over.

Note: You can add other sprouts to this omelet recipe, but if you add smaller sprouts, such as alfalfa sprouts, sauté the other vegetable one to three minutes before adding the alfalfa sprouts. Add the alfalfa last so that they cook for only two minutes. Then, add all the vegetables, including the alfalfa sprouts, to the egg as in step 7 above.

Breakfast Crepe with Sprouts

This recipe offers very basic instructions on how to make crepes and a suggestion about a healthy breakfast filling. The great thing about knowing how to make a simple crepe is that you can fill it with just about anything and it can be a food for any time of day.

This recipe yields six servings.

Ingredients

For the batter
1 cup flour

½ tsp. salt

1 cup milk

3 eggs

4 (or more) Tbsp. melted butter

For the filling
1½ lbs. flank steak

4 Tbsp. melted butter

2 cups mung bean sprouts

1 finely diced green bell pepper

½ cup finely chopped mushrooms

8 oz. cream cheese

12 crepes

Directions

To prepare crepes:
1. Sift together flour and salt.
2. In a separate bowl, whisk the milk and eggs together.
3. Add the flour/salt to the milk/egg mixture a little at a time, beating the batter each time you add flour.
4. After all the flour is added to the milk/egg mixture, add 2 Tbsp. of melted butter.
5. Allow batter to rest in refrigerator for two to eight hours (You can make this batter the night before.)
6. Melt 2 Tbsp. of butter in a skillet over a medium-high heat.

7. After the butter has melted, pour the butter off into a small glass bowl, leaving a well-buttered skillet. (You will be using the butter you poured off.)

8. Transfer your crepe batter into a container that you can pour from (A small pitcher or a large measuring cup is ideal for this.)

9. Slowly pour about 3 Tbsp. batter onto the hot skillet.

10. Lift the skillet and move it in such a way as to spread the batter out evenly to form a thin, round "pancake."

11. As the thin layer of batter starts to bubble (after about a minute), flip the crepe and cook the other side.

12. After you flip the crepe, allow the crepe to cook about another minute.

13. Transfer the cooked crepe to a warm plate.

14. Brush the surface of the hot skillet with melted butter (You can use a pastry brush or a rolled up paper towel.)

15. Repeat steps 9 through 13 to use the rest of the batter.

16. You can stack the crepes on the warm plate.

This recipe should yield about a dozen crepes.

To prepare filling:

17. Slice flank steak into strips as thin as you possibly can and then into bite-size pieces.

18. Melt 4 Tbsp. butter over medium heat in the same skillet you used to cook the crepes.

19. Brown meat in melted butter over medium-high heat.

20. Add the bean sprouts, green bell pepper, and mushrooms to the skillet with the flank steak.

21. Cook ingredients together for about three minutes, until steak is done.

22. Spread a crepe with 2 tsp. of cream cheese.

23. Spoon about ¼ cup of steak and sprout mixture onto the cream cheese-covered crepe.

24. Roll the crepe around the filling.

Transfer, seam side down, to a serving plate and serve warm.

Lentil Sprout Lasagna with Marinara

This recipe yields six to eight servings.

Ingredients for the lasagna

1 (8 oz.) package no-cook lasagna noodles

1 large eggplant, peeled and sliced thin

3 cups of lentil sprouts

1 15-oz. can tomato sauce

1 6-oz. can tomato paste

2 eggs

1½ cups ricotta cheese

½ cup Parmesan cheese

Fresh ground pepper (to taste)

1 lb. mushrooms

1 diced green bell pepper

1 Tbsp. olive oil

3 cups lentil sprouts

2 cups Mozzarella cheese

Ingredients for the marinara

1 15-oz. can whole tomatoes sliced into small pieces (½-inch chunks)

1 15-oz. can tomato sauce

1 6-oz. can tomato paste

2 crushed cloves garlic

1 finely diced medium red onion

1 cup crushed walnuts

1 tsp. dried basil

1 tsp. dried oregano

Salt (to taste)

Directions

To prepare the marinara:

1. Pour tomatoes, tomato sauce, tomato paste, garlic, onion, walnuts, basil, oregano, and salt in a medium sauce pan.
2. Cook over medium heat for one hour.

To prepare the fillings:

3. Lightly salt the eggplant slices.
4. Place sliced eggplant under broiler a few minutes until it starts to sweat. (Beads of moisture will appear on the outer surface of the eggplant).
5. Turn eggplant slices over once and broil the other side for about two minutes.
6. Remove eggplant slices from broiler and place on paper towel.
7. Place ricotta cheese in a bowl with two eggs, Parmesan cheese, and fresh ground black pepper to taste.
8. Use a whisk to mix ricotta cheese mixture well.
9. In a sauté pan, lightly sauté mushrooms with green bell pepper in olive oil until the pepper is slightly soft.
10. Place lentil sprouts, 15 oz.-can of tomato sauce, and 6 oz.-can tomato paste in food processor with steel S-blades.
11. Pulse lightly about ten times.

Putting it all together:

12. Preheat oven to 350 degrees.

13. In 9-inch by 13-inch casserole or baking dish, alternate layers, beginning with ½ cup marinara in bottom of pan.

14. Place single layer of lasagna noodles over marinara in bottom of pan.

15. Place eggplant on top of first layer of lasagna noodles.

16. Spoon half the prepared sautéed mushrooms and peppers on top of eggplant.

17. Spoon half of the ricotta mixture on top of sautéed mushrooms.

18. Spoon about ½ cup marinara over ricotta mixture.

19. Lay a second layer of lasagna noodles over gravy.

20. Spoon lentil sprout filling on top of the second layer of lasagna noodles.

21. Spoon remainder of sautéed mushrooms and peppers on top of lentil mixture.

22. Spoon remainder ricotta mixture on top of sautéed mushrooms.

23. Cover ricotta mixture with 1 cup Mozzarella cheese.

24. Lay a third layer of lasagna noodles over Mozzarella cheese.

25. Spoon about ½ to 1 cup marinara over lasagna noodles.

26. Put remainder of Mozzarella cheese on top.

27. Cover baking dish with aluminum foil.

28. Bake for 30 to 35 minutes.

29. Remove foil and bake another 15 minutes or until cheese starts to brown.

The next four recipes are dishes referred to as pie. The first recipe uses a traditional pie crust that could just as well be used in any fruit pie. The two recipes that follow that are shepherd's pies that use a mashed potato as a top "crust." The final recipe is a pizza pie.

Pork and Bean Sprout Pie

This recipe will give you eight servings.

Ingredients

For pastry

2 cups white unbleached flour

1 tsp. salt

⅔ cup shortening (butter, solid vegetable shortening, or lard)

4 to 8 Tbsp. cold water

For filling

1½ cups chicken broth

3 Tbsp. flour

1 chopped medium yellow onion

½ seeded and diced large green bell pepper 2 thinly sliced celery ribs

1 crushed garlic clove

2 Tbsp. butter

½ cup water

2 Tbsp. soy sauce

½ tsp. salt

Dash of pepper

3 cups diced roast pork

1½ cups mung bean sprouts

½ cup sliced water chestnuts

Directions

For pastry

1. Sift together flour and salt.
2. Place flour, salt, and shortening in the bowl of a food processor.

3. Pulse about ten times until the mixture has a coarse crumb consistency.

4. Transfer the mixture to a bowl.

5. Add 2 Tbsp. cold water to flour and shortening mixture.

6. Use a fork or pastry cutter to work the cold water into the flour and shortening mixture.

7. Add another 2 Tbsp. cold water to flour and shortening mixture.

8. Use a fork or pastry cutter to work the cold water into the flour and shortening mixture.

9. Add 1 Tbsp. cold water to flour and shortening mixture.

10. Use a fork or pastry cutter to work the cold water into the flour and shortening mixture.

11. Continue to add cold water in this manner until you can gather pastry into a ball that does not crumb apart.

12. Divide the pastry into two sections and wrap each section in plastic wrap and chill while you prepare the filling.

For filling

13. Put the chicken broth in a small sauce pan.

14. Put the saucepan of broth on the stove top on a medium heat.

15. Use a whisk to incorporate the flour into the chicken broth.

16. Add salt and pepper to taste.

17. Stir constantly until the mixture starts to bubble.

18. Remove saucepan from heat and stir occasionally while you prepare the vegetables.

19. In a large skillet over a medium-high heat, sauté onion, green pepper, celery, and garlic in butter until soft.

20. Stir prepared chicken gravy, water, soy sauce, salt, pepper, pork, bean sprouts, and water chestnuts into skillet containing vegetables.

21. Heat skillet ingredients until they begin to boil, stirring occasionally.
22. Remove from heat.

Putting it all together

23. Preheat oven to 400 degrees.
24. Remove one pastry ball from refrigerator.
25. Spread flour over a large flat work surface.
26. Remove pastry from plastic wrap.
27. Press pastry flat on floured surface with your hands.
28. Use a rolling pin to roll pastry to ⅛-inch thickness and a little larger than a 9-inch pie plate.
29. Roll pastry onto the rolling pin.
30. Unroll pastry into 9-inch pie plate.
31. Push pastry down to form in pie plate.
32. Spoon filling into pastry in pie plate.
33. Remove second pastry from plastic wrap.
34. Repeat steps 27 through 29.
35. Unroll pastry onto top of filled pie plate.
36. Trim around edges of pie plate, leaving about ¼ inch excess.
37. Tuck top pastry under bottom pastry around edges of pie and seal by pinching all around.
38. Cut several slits in top of pie to let steam escape.
39. Bake at 400 degrees for 45 minutes to an hour or until pastry is golden.
40. Remove from oven and allow 15 minutes to cool before serving.

Vegetarian Shepherd's Pie

This recipe will serve eight.

Ingredients

1 Tbsp. olive oil

5 crushed garlic cloves

1 coarsely chopped red bell pepper

1 coarsely chopped green bell pepper

2 thinly sliced medium-size zucchini

1 cup crushed canned tomatoes

¼ tsp. salt

⅛ tsp. fresh ground black pepper

2 cups cooked sprouted black beans

2 cups cooked sprouted chickpeas

3 cups mashed sweet potatoes

¼ tsp. paprika (optional garnish)

Directions for cooking sprouted black beans and chickpeas

1. Put 8 cups of water, 1 cup sprouted black beans, and 1 cup sprouted chick peas in a large pot.
2. Bring water, sprouted black beans, and sprouted chick peas to a boil.
3. Reduce water to a simmer.
4. Cook sprouted black beans and sprouted chick peas for about ten minutes until soft.
5. Drain cooked sprouted black beans and sprouted chick peas in a colander.

Ingredients for mashed sweet potatoes

4 peeled large sweet potatoes

1 stick butter

1 Tbsp. and ½ tsp. salt

¼ tsp. fresh ground black pepper (optional)

½ tsp. cayenne pepper (more or less, to taste)

Directions for mashed potatoes

1. Peel sweet potatoes and cut into quarters.
2. Place quartered sweet potatoes in a 3- to 4-quart pot.
3. Cover sweet potatoes with about 2 quarts cold water.
4. Add 1 Tbsp. salt to water.
5. Place pot with sweet potatoes and water on stove top over a medium-high heat.
6. Bring water to a rolling boil.
7. Reduce heat to medium low.
8. Simmer for about 20 minutes until fully tender.
9. After 20 minutes, test sweet potatoes with a fork to see if they are fully tender.
10. When the sweet potatoes are tender, remove from heat.
11. Drain sweet potatoes into a colander.
12. Add butter to bottom of the still-warm pot the sweet potatoes cooked in.
13. Stir the butter until it is melted.
14. Return the sweet potatoes to the butter in the still-warm pot they cooked in.
15. Return the pot to the burner it cooked on, though the burner should be off or on very low heat.
16. Use a potato masher to mash the sweet potatoes with the butter.
17. Add salt, fresh ground black pepper, and cayenne pepper to taste.
18. If the potatoes are dry, you may add a splash of milk.

Directions for filling and putting it together

19. Preheat the oven to 375 degrees.

20. Heat 2 tsp. of the oil in a medium skillet over medium heat for one minute.
21. Add 2 cloves of the garlic to skillet and sauté for one minute.
22. Add the red bell pepper, green bell pepper, and zucchini and sauté, stirring occasionally, for three to four minutes or until crisp-tender.
23. Add ¾ cup of the crushed tomatoes, salt, and fresh ground black pepper.
24. Cook uncovered for five minutes.
25. Place the cooked sprouted black beans, cooked sprouted chickpeas, and the remaining oil, garlic, and tomatoes in the bowl of a food processor and puree until smooth (about 30 seconds).
26. Spoon the puree into a lightly greased 9-inch pie pan.
27. Top the puree with the skillet vegetable mixture.
28. Spoon the mashed potatoes on top.
29. Bake, uncovered, for 25 minutes or until the potatoes are lightly browned.
30. Sprinkle with paprika if desired.

Shepherd's Pie with Meat

This recipe is somewhat similar to the vegetarian shepherd's pie recipe except that it calls for regular potatoes, ground beef, and sprouted barley. You can, of course, substitute many of the ingredients in this casserole-like dish. Try adding green beans or using the sweet potato layer instead of the regular potato layer. Any way you make it, it is delicious.

This recipe yields eight servings.

Ingredients
1 Tbsp. olive oil
5 crushed garlic cloves

1 lb. lean ground beef

1 coarsely chopped red bell pepper

1 coarsely chopped green bell pepper

2 thinly sliced medium-size zucchinis

1 cup crushed canned tomatoes

1 cup sprouted barley

¼ tsp. salt

⅛ tsp. fresh ground black pepper

1 cup cooked sprouted chickpeas

3 cups mashed sweet potatoes

¼ tsp. paprika (optional garnish)

Directions for cooking sprouted and chickpeas

1. Put 4 cups of water and 1 cup sprouted chickpeas and in a pot.
2. Bring water and sprouted chickpeas to a boil.
3. Reduce water to a simmer.
4. Cook sprouted chickpeas for about ten minutes until soft.
5. Drain cooked sprouted chickpeas in a colander.

Ingredients for mashed potatoes

4 peeled large potatoes (red potatoes or russet potatoes are good here)

1 stick butter

1 Tbsp. and ½ tsp. salt

¼ tsp. fresh ground black pepper (optional)

½ cup whole milk or cream (more or less, to taste or dryness of potatoes)

Directions for mashed sweet potatoes

1. Peel potatoes and cut into quarters.
2. Place quartered potatoes in a 3- to 4-quart pot.
3. Cover potatoes with about 2 quarts cold water.
4. Add 1 Tbsp. salt to water.

5. Place pot with potatoes and water on stove top over a medium-high heat.
6. Bring water to a rolling boil.
7. Reduce heat to medium low.
8. Simmer for about 20 minutes until potatoes are fully tender.
9. After 20 minutes, test potatoes with a fork to see if they are fully tender. When the potatoes are tender, remove from heat.
10. Drain potatoes into a colander.
11. Add butter to bottom of the still-warm pot the potatoes cooked in.
12. Stir the butter until it is melted.
13. Return the potatoes to the pot they cooked in.
14. Return the pot to the burner it cooked on, though the burner should be off or on very low heat.
15. Use a potato masher to mash the potatoes with the butter. (Alternatively, you can use a hand mixer to give you a very smoothly mashed potato.)
16. Warm milk or cream on the stovetop or microwave.
17. Slowly add warmed milk or cream to potatoes as you mash them.
18. Add salt and fresh ground black pepper to taste.
19. If the potatoes are dry, add a splash more milk.
20. Keep potatoes warm on warmed stovetop.

Directions for filling and putting it together
21. Preheat the oven to 375 degrees.
22. Heat 2 tsp. of the oil in a large skillet over medium heat for one minute.
23. Add 2 cloves of the garlic to skillet and sauté for one minute.
24. Add ground beef to skillet and cook until brown (about ten minutes).
25. Stir ground beef occasionally while cooking.

26. Add the red bell pepper, green bell pepper, and zucchini and sauté, stirring occasionally, for three to four minutes or until crisp-tender.

27. Add ¾ cup of the crushed tomatoes, sprouted barley, salt, and fresh ground black pepper.

28. Cook uncovered for five minutes.

29. Place the cooked sprouted chickpeas and the remaining oil, garlic, and tomatoes in the bowl of a food processor and puree until smooth (about 30 seconds).

30. Spoon the puree into a lightly greased 9-inch pie pan.

31. Top the puree with the skillet beef and vegetable mixture.

32. Spoon the mashed potatoes on top.

33. Bake, uncovered, for 25 minutes or until the potatoes are lightly browned.

34. Sprinkle with paprika if desired.

Sprouted Pesto Pizza

The recipe is for a pizza topped with pesto. You may, however, top the pizza with whatever you choose. Pizza is a wonderful dish to experiment with.

You will make this recipe in stages. First, you will prepare the dough for the crust. You will then prepare a soaked cashew spread that is similar in consistency to ricotta cheese. After you make the cashew spread, you will prepare the pesto. Finally, you will put it all together to make the pizza.

This recipe will make one large thin-crust pizza.

The Crust

Ingredients

1 cup warm water (105 to 110 degrees)

1 package active dry yeast

1 tsp. salt

2 Tbsp. olive oil

1 cup sprouted wheat or barley

Approximately 4 cups of unbleached white flour

Directions

1. Proof the yeast in the warm water. (To proof the yeast, put the warm water into a large mixing bowl and scatter the yeast over the surface of the water. Allow the yeast to sit undisturbed for about five minutes. At this point you will start to see the yeast "explode" in the water. The slight bubbling tells you that the yeast is active.)

2. Add salt and whisk well.

3. Add olive oil and whisk well.

4. Add sprouted wheat or barley and whisk well.

5. Add flour ½ cup at a time, whisking and mixing well with each addition. The more flour you add, the thicker and stickier the dough will become.

6. As the dough becomes too thick to mix with the whisk, use a large wooden spoon to incorporate the flour.

7. Add flour until the dough starts to come away from the side of the bowl.

8. Spread flour on a flat work surface.

9. Transfer the sticky dough to the floured work surface.

10. Knead the dough by hand just until you can hold it in your hand for five seconds without having the dough stick to your hands.

11. Prepare a separate bowl by covering the interior surface of the bowl with a coat of olive oil.

12. Place the dough in the prepared bowl and turn it over once. Turning the dough over gives the top of the dough a thin coat of olive oil and prevents it from becoming dry as the dough rises.

13. Cover the bowl with a lid or a dishcloth and allow the dough to rise in a warm place for an hour or until the dough has doubled in size.

14. After the dough has risen, punch it down in the bowl and turn it back out onto your work surface.

15. Knead the dough for one minute.

16. Return the dough to the bowl it rose in and cover it.

17. Place the bowl of dough in the refrigerator and allow it to cool.

18. Check the dough after 90 minutes. If it has risen to the top of the bowl, punch it down again and return it to the refrigerator.

Soaked Cashew Spread

Ingredients

1 cup raw cashews that have been soaked for four to six hours

2 Tbsp. fresh squeezed lemon juice

½ tsp. salt

⅓ cup water

Directions

1. Place soaked cashews, lemon juice, salt, and half of the water in the bowl of a food processor

2. Pulse to blend the mixture until it reaches the texture of ricotta cheese. You can add more water as needed.

3. Set mixture aside in a small bowl.

Pesto

Ingredients

1 cup packed fresh basil (or spinach may be used)

1 medium clove of garlic

1 Tbsp. extra virgin olive oil

2 Tbsp. raw pine nuts (try black walnuts for a bolder flavor)

1 Tbsp. fresh squeezed lemon juice

½ tsp. sea salt

2 Tbsp. finely grated Parmesan cheese

Directions

1. Place all ingredients except the Parmesan cheese in the bowl of a food processor.
2. Run food processor for about 30 seconds until the basil has combined with the other ingredients to form a thick paste.
3. Transfer basil mixture to a small bowl.
4. Add Parmesan cheese to basil mixture and stir in to incorporate.
5. Set aside (or refrigerate if not using immediately).

Putting it all together for a pizza

Ingredients

Dough for crust

Soaked cashew spread

Pesto

Olive oil (about 1 Tbsp.)

Kosher salt (a sprinkling)

One thinly sliced tomato

One small, thinly sliced onion

1 to 2 cups Mozzarella cheese

Note: The topping are only suggestions; try black olives, roasted red peppers, or whatever pizza topping you and your family enjoy.

Directions

1. Preheat oven to 400 degrees.
2. Prepare a pizza pan (a large flat baking dish) by lightly coating it with olive oil and a thin dusting of corn meal.
3. Remove dough for crust from refrigerator and turn out onto a lightly floured work surface.
4. Use your hands to punch the dough down and begin to shape as desired.
5. Work the dough with your hands or a roller to shape dough into the desired size and thickness.
6. Transfer shaped dough to prepared pizza pan.
7. Place dough in preheated oven and bake for five to seven minutes.
8. Remove crust from oven and allow it to cool for five minutes.
9. Brush top of crust with a thin coating of olive oil.
10. Lightly sprinkle kosher salt top of crust.
11. Spread pesto mixture evenly over top of pizza.
12. Spread soaked cashew mixture on top of pesto.
13. Arrange tomatoes on top of cashew mixture.
14. Spread Mozzarella cheese on top of pizza.
15. Arrange onion on top of pizza.
16. Put pizza in oven and bake until cheese and crust edges start to brown (about 15 minutes).
17. Remove from oven and allow 5 minutes to cool slightly before slicing to serve.

Samosa

Samosas are filled pastries that are Indian in origin. They are a savory snack that is usually fried. Whether you are in Mumbai, London, or New York, samosas can often be found and purchased fresh and hot from street vendors. Traditionally, samosas are filled with meat, potatoes, and a legume of some sort, such as peas. This version uses a ricotta cheese pastry and is baked rather than fried. This recipe will yield about 12 samosas.

Ingredients

Ricotta cheese pastry

8 oz. ricotta cheese

1 cup unsalted cultured butter, softened

2 cups all-purpose flour

¼ tsp. kosher salt

Sweet potato filling

¼ cup olive oil

1 chopped large onion

2 Tbsp. fresh squeezed lime juice

1 tsp. grated fresh ginger

1 crushed garlic clove garlic

½ tsp. salt

¼ tsp. ground cardamom

3 baked, peeled, and mashed medium sweet potatoes

1 cup chopped sprouted mung beans

Green dipping sauce (optional)

1 cup yogurt

½ cup loosely packed cilantro leaves

½ cup fresh mint leaves

½ cup alfalfa sprouts

1 seeded and chopped jalapeño pepper

2 cloves garlic

Salt (to taste)

Directions

For the pastry:
1. Use a stand or hand mixer to beat the ricotta.
2. Beat ricotta cheese and butter together until smooth.
3. Beat the salt into the ricotta cheese and butter.
4. Add the flour ¼ cup at a time to the ricotta cheese and butter until the mixture comes together in a ball.
5. Wrap the ball of pastry in plastic.
6. Flatten the plastic-wrapped pastry and refrigerate it for at least one hour.

For the sweet potato and sprouted mung bean filling:
1. Pour olive oil into a skillet and heat over medium heat.
2. Add the onion to skillet and sauté onion until it is just soft (about five minutes).
3. Add the lime juice, chopped sprouted mung beans, ginger, garlic, salt, and cardamom to skillet.
4. Continue cooking for two minutes.
5. Transfer the mixture from skillet to a bowl.
6. Add mashed sweet potato to onion mixture and mix well.
7. Set aside to cool (if the sweet potato filling is warm, the pastry will be too difficult to work with).
8. Preheat the oven to 375 degrees.
9. Line a baking sheet with parchment paper or waxed paper.
10. Lightly flour a flat working surface.
11. Turn the pastry dough out onto the floured work surface.

12. Roll the dough on the floured surface to about ⅛-inch thick.

13. Use a round cookie cutter or biscuit cutter (about 3-inches wide) to cut circles in the dough (cut the circles as close together as you can to get as many circles as possible).

14. Set cut pastry circles aside in the refrigerator.

15. Gather up the unused pastry dough and roll it out again to about ⅛ inch thick.

16. Continue to cut circles in this manner until you have used all the pastry dough.

17. Chill cut pastry circles for about 20 minutes.

18. After they have chilled, remove cut pastry circles from the refrigerator a few at a time.

19. Place 1 Tbsp. of the sweet potato/mung bean filling in the center of a dough circle.

20. Fold the circle in half to form a half-moon shape.

21. Seal the edges of the pastry together.

22. Place the samosa on the parchment-lined baking sheet.

23. Repeat with remaining filling and dough.

24. Bake the samosas for about 20 minutes until the edges are lightly golden.

For the dipping sauce:

25. Combine all sauce ingredients in a food processor or blender and blend until smooth.

Serve the samosas warm with sauce for dipping

Sweet and Nutty Sweet Potatoes

This recipe will serve four.

Ingredients

2 medium sweet potatoes

3 sliced medium carrots

¼ cup pine nuts

½ cup crushed fresh, frozen, or canned crushed pineapple with juice

½ tsp. cinnamon

½ cup mung beans sprouts

Directions

1. Preheat oven to 400 degrees.
2. Pierce sweet potatoes in several places with fork and place them in a shallow baking dish.
3. Place sweet potatoes in oven and baked 45 minutes.
4. Remove sweet potatoes from oven and allow them to cool.
5. Cut cooled sweet potatoes into ½-inch cubes.
6. Put cubed sweet potatoes in a medium bowl and set aside.
7. Put sliced carrots into a vegetable steamer and steam for eight minutes.
8. Transfer steamed carrots to bowl with sweet potatoes.
9. Add remaining ingredients to the bowl with sweet potatoes and carrots and mix well.

Serve chilled or at room temperature.

Sprout-stuffed Red Peppers

This can be an excellent vegetarian main course or a hearty side dish with fish or fowl. This recipe yields four servings.

Ingredients

1 gallon water

4 red bell peppers

1 Tbsp. salt

¼ cup butter

1 large minced red onion

¾ cup uncooked long-grain white rice

1 cup sprouted quinoa

½ lb. chopped mushrooms

1 cup finely chopped celery

¼ cup finely chopped carrots

¼ cup corn (fresh or frozen)

1 cup finely chopped spinach

2 cloves finely chopped garlic

¼ tsp. cayenne pepper

1 large peeled and finely chopped tomato (The trick to peeling a tomato is to score an "x" on the bottom, put them in a bowl, and pour boiling water over them. Allow the tomatoes to sit in hot water for a minute. When you pour the water off, you will be able to easily pull the peel off of the tomato's peel.)

½ cup fresh grated Parmesan cheese

Directions

1. Preheat oven to 350 degrees.

2. Add 1 gallon of water and 1 Tbsp. salt to a large soup pot and bring the water to a boil.

3. As the water is heating, cut the tops off of the peppers, remove the seeds, and finely chop up the flesh removed fromaround the stem. Reserve the flesh chopped from around the stem.

4. When the water boils, add the hollowed peppers to the water.

5. Cook the peppers for about four minutes, or until the peppers start to get soft.

6. Remove the peppers from the water.

7. Save the water and set aside.

8. Place the peppers in a colander to drain and cool.

9. In a medium sauce pan, heat 2 Tbsp. butter over a medium-high heat and allow butter to melt.

10. Add chopped red onions to butter and sauté them until they are soft.

11. Add uncooked rice to sautéed onions and stir.

12. Cook the rice, stirring frequently, for about ten minutes.

13. Add 1½ cups of the water you cooked the peppers in to the rice/onion mixture.

14. Bring water to a boil.

15. Cover pan and turn heat down to low.

16. Cook rice on low heat for about 20 minutes, or until the rice absorbs all the water.

17. As the rice cooks, melt 2 Tbsp. butter in a medium to large sauté pan over medium-high heat.

18. Add the chopped tops of the peppers, mushrooms, celery, carrots, corn, spinach, garlic, and cayenne to the pan.

19. Sauté all vegetable for about ten minutes, or until tender.

20. In a large bowl, combine cooked rice, sautéed vegetables, sprouted quinoa, tomato, and half of the Parmesan cheese.

21. Season mixture with salt and pepper to taste.

22. Stuff each of the hollowed pepper shells with rice/quinoa/vegetable mixture.

23. Place stuffed peppers in a 9-inch by 9-inch baking dish.

24. Topped stuffed peppers with remaining Parmesan cheese.

25. If you have any remaining stuffing, you can put it around the bases of the peppers in the baking dish.

26. Bake at 350 degrees for 20 to 30 minutes.

Stuffed Zucchini

This makes an excellent side dish or vegetarian main course and will yield two to four servings.

Ingredients

1 large zucchini

1½ cups sprouted sunflower seeds

½ cup cooked wild rice

¼ cup fresh grated Parmesan cheese

1½ tsp. olive oil

½ cup finely chopped white onion

1 rib finely chopped celery

½ cup dried bread crumbs

Salt (to taste)

Butter (to taste)

Directions

1. Cut the zucchini in half lengthwise.
2. Preheat oven to 350 degrees.
3. Cut or scoop out the center of each half of the zucchini. Be careful not to puncture through to the bottom or side of the zucchini. Do not worry if you puncture the skin of the zucchini as you can still use the vegetable if it is punctured. It makes for a nicer presentation if you avoid doing so.
4. Set the zucchini that was removed from the halves aside in a bowl.
5. Place the hollowed out zucchini shells, cut side up, in a baking dish.
6. Finely chop the zucchini pieces that were scooped out of the shells and place them in a mixing bowl.

7. Add sprouted sunflower seeds, wild rice, and Parmesan cheese to the zucchini in the mixing bowl.
8. Fold the zucchini, sunflower seeds, wild rice, and Parmesan cheese gently together.
9. Pour olive oil into a skillet and heat olive oil over medium heat.
10. Add onion and celery to olive oil.
11. Sauté onion and celery, stirring constantly, until the onion is soft.
12. Add bread crumbs and salt to onion and celery.
13. Continue stirring onion and celery mixture for another minute.
14. Add onion and celery mixture to zucchini, sunflower seeds, wild rice, and Parmesan cheese in mixing bowl.
15. Gently fold items in mixing bowl together.
16. Spoon mixture from mixing bowl into hollowed zucchini shells.
17. Cover stuffed zucchini in baking dish with aluminum foil.
18. Bake at 350 degrees for 45 minutes.
19. Remove foil.
20. Place a small dot of butter on each zucchini half.
21. Return zucchini to oven and continue to bake for 15 minutes, or until the filling is brown or the zucchini is tender.

Wild Rice Stuffing

This recipe is guaranteed to be the hit of any holiday meal. After making it once, you may want to increase the recipe to satisfy all those who demand more of it and leftovers. This recipe will serve about ten people.

Ingredients

5 cups sprouted wild rice (Soak the rice in water for two days and change the water after the first day.)
1 cup sprouted sunflower seeds
1½ cups chopped celery

1 cup chopped apple

1 cup parsley, chopped

1 cup wild black walnuts or regular walnuts

¾ cup red onion, minced

½ cup raisins

½ cup chopped dates

½ cup chopped dried apricots

½ cup dried cranberries

½ cup chopped candied ginger

1 to 2 cups cubed wheat berry sunflower bread or sprouted oatmeal
bread (*see Chapter 12*)

½ to 1 cup chicken stock

½ cup chopped fresh sage or 3 Tbsp. dried sage

½ cup chopped fresh thyme or 3 Tbsp. dried thyme

1 Tbsp. kosher salt

Fresh ground black pepper (to taste)

Directions

1. Combine all ingredients in a large mixing bowl.

2. You can stuff poultry with this delicious stuffing and/or put it in
   a well-buttered casserole dish.

3. Heat the rice in a casserole dish in the oven at 350 degrees for
   about 45 minutes.

Baked Beats with Chive Sprouts

Give beets a chance. This is a wonderful recipe that can be made fat
(with sour cream) or skinny (with non-fat yogurt). The fat recipe will
remind you of hot borscht, the wonderful beet soup of Eastern Euro-
pean and Russian origin. This recipe will give you six to eight servings.

Ingredients

6 large beets

1½ cups sour cream or non-fat yogurt

½ cup chive sprouts

Salt (to taste)

Fresh ground black pepper (to taste)

Directions

1. Preheat oven to 425 degrees.
2. Wrap each individual beet in aluminum foil.
3. Bake beets for one hour, or until tender.
4. Allow beets to cool to the point when you can handle them.
5. As the beets cool, whisk together remaining ingredients.
6. Remove foil from beets.
7. Remove skin from beets with paring knife.
8. Mash beets or simply cut in half or in quarters.
9. Serve with sour cream or yogurt sprout mixture.

Baked Vegetables with Bacon

This yields four to six servings.

Ingredients

1 small cabbage

3 carrots, quartered

3 peeled and cubed medium-sized sweet potatoes

4 onions, quartered

1 cup mung bean sprouts

4 strips bacon, half cooked

Salt to taste

Fresh ground black pepper

Directions

1. Preheat oven to 350 degrees.
2. Cut cabbage into eight sections.
3. Arrange cabbage in well-buttered 1½-quart baking dish.
4. Between cabbage sections, place carrots, sweet potatoes, and onions.
5. Pour ½ inch of water in bottom of baking dish.
6. Cover baking dish and bake for 30 minutes.
7. Add mung bean sprouts.
8. Season with salt and pepper to taste.
9. Cover with aluminum foil and bake an additional 15 minutes, or until vegetables are tender.
10. Remove from oven and uncover.
11. Place bacon strips on top on the cabbage and return to oven.
12. Bake until bacon is done.

Serve this dish hot.

Green Peas with Mustard Sprouts

This dish will give you eight servings.

Ingredients

12 cloves pressed garlic

1-inch piece of peeled and chopped ginger root

1½ cups vegetable stock (chicken stock will work as well)

1 tsp. ground cumin

4 Tbsp. peanut oil

2 tsp. whole cumin seed

1 whole ancho chile pepper

3 peeled and finely chopped medium tomatoes (The trick to peeling a tomato is to score an "x" on the bottom, put them in a bowl, and pour boiling water over them. Allow the tomatoes to sit in hot water for a minute. When you pour the water off, you will be able to easily pull the peel off of the tomato.)

2 tsp. ground coriander

1½ lbs. (about 8 cups) green beans, cut in half

1½ tsp. salt

3 Tbsp. lemon juice

2 cups mustard seed sprouts

Fresh ground black pepper (to taste)

Directions

1. Place the garlic, ginger, and ½ cup vegetable stock in the bowl of a food processor and process the ingredients until smooth.
2. Heat a large wok over medium heat.
3. When wok is hot, add ground cumin to the dry wok for just a few seconds to toast.
4. Remove the cumin from the wok after a few seconds and place it in a small dish. Set toasted cumin aside. Use a paper towel to wipe the remaining cumin from the wok.
5. Return wok to medium heat and add peanut oil to the wok.
6. When the oil is hot, add cumin seeds.
7. After ten seconds, add ancho chile pepper to wok.
8. After another 20 seconds, add the garlic and ginger paste.
9. Stir the ingredients over the medium heat for about two minutes.
10. Add tomatoes and coriander.
11. Stir the ingredients over the medium heat for about two minutes.
12. Add green beans, salt, and remaining vegetable stock.
13. Stir mixture constantly until it comes to a boil.
14. Turn the heat down to low and cover the wok.
15. Allow beans to cook five to ten minutes, stirring once or twice during this time.

16. When the beans are tender, remove cover from wok.
17. Add toasted cumin and lemon juice.
18. Return heat to medium and allow mixture to boil.
19. Stir the mixture occasionally.
20. Allow most of the liquid to cook off.
21. Remove wok form heat.

Serve over rice with a generous portion of mustard seed sprouts on top.

Many of the recipes included here as side dishes can be considered main dishes because they are hearty and tasty. The stuffed peppers and zucchini are classic dishes that you can experiment with endlessly. The sprouts you use in any of these dishes can be substituted for other sprouts that strike your fancy.

Chapter 12

Breads, Baked Goods, and Cereal

Arguably, bread and baked goods are some of the most rewarding food items that can come out of your kitchen and the same is true with bread and baked goods made with sprouts. The recipes here range from the ancient whole-sprout recipe of Essene bread to the sweet and scrumptious sprouted pumpkin cinnamon rolls. Do not miss trying your hand at anything in this chapter. The breads will have your family and friends demanding your baked goods at every meal.

Essene Bread

No sprout recipe book would be complete without a recipe for Essene bread. The basic Essene bread recipe has been around for thousands of years. It is highly nutritious and can be made without using an oven. The bread originated in the desert cultures of the Middle East. Because it is cooked at a very low temperature, it is possible to bake this bread in the hot sun. Essene bread is very similar to the recipe for Just Barley Bread in that it can have very few ingredients and can be made without yeast. There are two Essene recipes here; the first is for a basic Essene bread and the second recipe takes the simple bread and turns it into a complex nutty wonder of sourdough, wheat, rye, and oats. Whether you plan on making the basic recipe or the sourdough recipe, plan on this bread taking you at least two days to make. The sour dough recipe can take as long as two weeks.

These recipes are so basic that they beg for experimentation. Use the recipes as a guide and then play around with them until you discover what works best for your tastes. This bread is great with a simple cheese spread such as cream cheese or quark.

Basic Mixed Grain Essene Bread

This recipe yields two loaves.

Ingredients
1 cup sprouted oats
1 cup sprouted rye
1 cup sprouted wheat
1 Tbsp. cornmeal

Directions
1. Drain soaked and sprouted grain well.
2. Place all soaked and sprouted grain in a food processor fitted with a stainless steel S-blade.
3. Pulse until the mixture resembles bread dough and forms a ball around the food processor blade.
4. Remove the ball of dough from the food processor and squeeze the moisture out of the dough.
5. Divide the dough into two equal rounds and lightly cover them with cornmeal.
6. Sprinkle a little cornmeal onto a baking sheet.
7. Place dough rounds on baking sheet.
8. Place dough rounds in oven.

9. Turn oven on to 160 degrees.

10. Bake for about an hour then turn your oven off.

11. Allow bread rounds to remain in oven for another 30 minutes.

12. Remove bread from oven and allow them to cool.

Essene bread should be stored in the refrigerator in an air-tight container. It will keep for up to a week.

Sourdough Essene Bread

Because you will be making this most basic of bread recipes, this sourdough recipe is the most basic of sourdough recipes. No yeast is required as you will be "capturing" the "wild" yeast that is present in the grains you use. With this sourdough recipe, you will be making a sourdough starter. A starter is a mixture that you will store in your refrigerator that can be used over and over again as you feed and replenish it with each use.

This recipe makes two loaves of sourdough Essene bread.

Ingredients

½ to 1 cup sourdough starter (flour and water)

1 cup sprouted oats

1 cup sprouted rye

1 cup sprouted wheat

¼ tsp. kosher salt

2 Tbsp. oil (canola or peanut) or melted butter

1 Tbsp. cornmeal

Directions

For the sourdough starter:

1. Mix 1 cup whole wheat flour with an equal amount of water in a small glass bowl.

2. Cover bowl with a top that allows the mixture to breathe, such as cheesecloth.

3. Allow flour and water mixture to sit at room temperature for 48 hours.

4. After 48 hours, add another ½ cup flour (white or whole wheat) and ½ cup water to flour and water mixture.

5. Allow to sit at room temperature for 48 hours with a loose cover of cheesecloth, plastic wrap, or a bowl lid.

6. On the fourth day, stir the flour and water mixture.

7. Remove half of the mixture and replace it with an equal amount of flour and water.

8. By day five, you may start to detect a sour smell and/or a bubbling in the mixture. This means that everything is going as it should.

9. Repeat steps 6 and 7 until your mixture starts to froth slightly. Once the mixture starts to froth, you have a sourdough starter.

10. Refrigerate your starter until you need to use it.

For the sourdough Essene bread:

11. The night before you make the bread, remove ½ cup of sourdough starter from the batch you made earlier.

12. Add ½ cup of flour and ½ cup of water to the ½ cup of starter you removed.

13. Allow this batch to sit at room temperature overnight.

14. In the morning, take ½ cup of the starter that sat out over night and add it to the original batch of starter.

15. Retain the other ½ cup of starter that sat out overnight for this recipe.

16. Place this ½ cup of starter in the bowl of a food processor fitted with a stainless steel S-blade.

17. Drain soaked and sprouted grain well.

18. Place all soaked and sprouted grain in a food processor with sour-dough starter.
19. Add ¼ tsp. kosher salt and oil or butter.
20. Pulse until the sprouted grains resemble bread dough and form a ball around the food processor blade.
21. Remove the ball of dough from the food processor.
22. Put a small amount of flour on a work surface and knead the dough for about five minutes.
23. Put the kneaded dough into a covered bowl and put it in the refrigerator for about 12 hours.
24. Remove dough from refrigerator and divide the dough into two equal rounds. Allow the rounds to sit in a warm place for two to three hours. (Inside your oven is a good place to let dough rest, as long as the oven is off.)
25. Preheat oven to 350 degrees. If you placed your dough in the oven to allow it to sit, make sure you remove the dough before turning your oven on.
26. Sprinkle a little cornmeal onto a baking sheet and place dough rounds on the baking sheet.
27. Place dough rounds in oven and bake them for 45 minutes at 350 degrees.
28. Remove bread rounds from oven and allow them to cool.

Essene bread should be stored in the refrigerator in an air-tight container. It will keep for up to a week.

Wheat Berry Sunflower Bread

This recipe yields two loaves.

Ingredients

1 package yeast

½ cup warm (90- to 100-degree) water

½ cup honey

2 tsp. coarse kosher salt

4 Tbsp. melted butter

2 cups warm (90- to 100-degree) buttermilk

1½ cups sprouted wheat berries

1½ cups sprouted sunflower seeds

4 cups (approximately) white unbleached flour

3½ cups (approximately) whole-wheat flour

Directions

1. In a large mixing bowl, proof yeast in warm water. To proof yeast, pour contents of yeast package into the warm water and allow it to sit for five to ten minutes. The yeast will start to become active as you will start to see small "explosions" in the water.
2. Whisk honey, salt, and melted butter into water/yeast mix.
3. Whisk in buttermilk.
4. Whisk in sprouted wheat berries and sunflower seeds.
5. Whisk in, 1 cup at a time, 3 cups of white unbleached flour. By this time the dough should start to get fairly stiff.
6. Using the dough hooks of an electric mixer, mix in the whole-wheat flour about ¼ cup at a time until the dough starts to come away from the sides of the bowl.
7. By hand, using a large spoon or spatula, mix in white unbleached flour until the dough starts to lose some of its stickiness.
8. Turn the dough out onto a floured surface and knead until the dough is soft, smooth, and not sticky.
9. Put the dough in a large buttered bowl, cover, and let it rise in a warm place until it doubles in size (which should take about an hour).
10. After the dough has risen, punch it down and turn it out onto a floured surface.
11. Cut the dough in half and shape into two loaves.

12. Place loaves into buttered 8.5-inch by 4.5-inch by 2.5-inch loaf pans.

13. Preheat oven to 375 degrees.

14. Cover loaves with a light towel and let rise until they are about 1 inch over the top of the pans.

15. Bake in a preheated oven at 375 degrees for about 45 minutes, and cover loosely with foil after about 25 minutes to keep the tops from getting too brown.

16. Remove from pans and cool them on racks immediately upon removing from oven.

Sprouted Oatmeal Bread

This bread is a meal in itself, but also makes great grilled cheese sandwiches. *Try using this bread with the grilled cheese recipe in Chapter 9.*

This recipe yields two loaves.

Ingredients

2 cups water

1 cup regular oatmeal (not quick-cooking oats)

4 Tbsp. butter

½ cup honey

1 package yeast

1 cup buttermilk

2 tsp. salt

1 cup sprouted oats

4 cups all-purpose flour

1 cup whole-wheat flour

Directions

1. Pour package of yeast into ½ cup of water warmed to 105 to 115 degrees in a small bowl. Allow to proof (which means to allow your yeast to sit in the warm water until it becomes active). You will notice the yeast begin to "explode" in the warm water.

2. Bring 1½ cups water to a rapid boil in a saucepan and stir in the oatmeal.

3. Once the water is boiling again, reduce the heat and cook oats for about three minutes until they start to thicken.

4. Remove saucepan of water from heat, stir in the butter and honey, and pour into a large bowl.

5. When mixture has cooled to 105 to 115 degrees, stir in the buttermilk and salt. (If you do not have an instant-read thermometer, use water that is just hot to your touch.)

6. Add the yeast and beat until smooth. Be sure the mixture is no more than 115 degrees when you add the yeast or it will kill off the yeast and your bread will not rise.

7. Stir in 2 cups of all-purpose flour and beat until smooth.

8. Stir in 1 cup of sprouted oats.

9. Add whole-wheat flour and beat until smooth. You can use a mixer fitted with dough hooks at this point if you have one and are inclined to do so.

10. Add more flour ½ cup at a time until the dough begins to pull away from the sides of the bowl. If you enjoy lighter bread, use more unbleached white flour. If you like your bread a little denser, use wheat.

11. Turn the dough onto a well-floured surface and knead just until the dough is no longer sticky.

12. Knead well until the dough becomes pliable and elastic. Add flour to the surface you are working on as necessary.

13. Spread butter over the inner surface of a large bowl and put the dough in it. Be sure the bowl is large enough to allow the dough to grow to twice its size. Turn the dough to cover its surface with the butter and cover the bowl.

14. Put the bowl in a warm place (room temperature) and allow it to rise until doubled in size.

15. Punch down and remove the dough to the lightly floured surface.

16. Knead the dough for about one minute and divide it in half, forming two equal loaves.

17. Butter two regular bread pans (about 9 by 4 by 3-inch) and put a loaf in each.

18. Cover with a towel and allow the loaves to rise until they are about 1 inch over the top of the pans.

19. While the bread is rising, preheat your oven to 375 degrees.

20. Put the pans into oven and bake for 40 to 45 minutes. Check brownness about 25 minutes into the baking. How brown or dark you want your bread to be is a personal preference. (If you would like to slow the browning of the bread, you can cover the loaves with aluminum foil.)

21. To test the bread, remove a loaf from the pan and tap on the bottom of it. The loaf should sound hollow when you tap on it.

22. Let the bread cool before slicing.

Just Barley Bread

This sprouted barley bread can also be made with sprouted wheat, buckwheat oats, or you can experiment with other grains. The recipe is exceedingly simple, nutritious, and incredibly delicious. The amazing thing about this recipe is that it is made with only two ingredients: barley and corn meal. You need to plan ahead three days before you make this, but you will be amazed by the results. Also, this is a recipe for those of you that love your slow cookers.

This bread is very dense, rich, delicious, and extra nutritious because it uses sprouted barley. The bread will keep in your refrigerator for about one week. This recipe will make one loaf.

Ingredients
1 cup unhulled barley berries (*see Chapter 4 for sprouting directions*)
⅛ cup corn meal

Directions
1. After sprouting the barley, drain the sprouts well before processing into dough. (You can choose not to rinse the barley after the sprouting is done.)
2. Place the sprouted barley berries into a food processor with the S-blade in place.
3. Pulse until the berries resemble bread dough and form a ball around the food processor blade.
4. Remove the ball of dough from the food processor.
5. Shape the dough into small ball and sprinkle it with corn meal.
6. Place the shaped dough into a small heat-proof glass bowl that will easily fit into your slow cooker.
7. Place the cover on your slow cooker.
8. Adjust slow cooker to low setting (do not use the "warm" setting but instead use the "low" setting. The warm setting is not warm enough).
9. Cook the bread for approximately eight to ten hours or until the bread is a deep dark brown.

The top of the bread may crack and it will have a tough, thick crust on the outside. The bread will have a moist texture on the inside.

Sprouted Grain Buttermilk Cakes

These pancakes are not only good, but good for you. You can add sprouted wheat, oats, rye, or sunflower seeds. You can make them even more delicious by adding blueberries to the batter.

This yields about 20 pancakes.

Ingredients

2½ cups unbleached all-purpose flour

½ cup whole wheat flour

½ cup to 1 cup sprouted wheat, oats, rye, or sunflower seeds (or a combination)

3 Tbsp. sugar (white or brown)

3 tsp. baking powder

1½ tsp. baking soda

¾ tsp. salt

3 eggs

3 cups buttermilk

¼ cup milk (whole, low-fat, or skim)

⅓ cup (5⅓Tbsp.) butter, melted

Directions

1. Heat a griddle or frying pans until it is hot.
2. Sift dry ingredients together (not sprouts).
3. Beat eggs and beat buttermilk into eggs.
4. Add sprouts to buttermilk/egg mixture.
5. Beat milk into wet mixture, then mix melted butter into wet mixture.
6. Add wet mixture to dry mixture just before you are ready to cook.
7. Stir the two mixtures to combine them. Stir just until the dry mixture is wet. Do not worry about lumps because they will cook out.

8. Spoon batter onto griddle or frying pan using about 2 Tbsp. of batter for each pancake. You can make the pancakes larger or smaller depending on your preference.
9. Flip the pancakes when bubbles start to appear on top.
10. Cook for about two more minutes. You can lift one to check how done the underside is.

Serve these pancakes hot. Pancakes that you do not eat can be frozen and reheated in a microwave, which is great for making a quick breakfast.

Thyme and Sprouted Sesame Bread

This is a variation on a Lebanese recipe called manaaeesh. If you have never had this, you are in for an addictive treat. Traditionally, this is Middle Eastern breakfast bread that goes great with a strong cup of coffee. You can, however, enjoy this treat at any time of day.

This recipe will make ten flatbreads.

Ingredients for the topping
2½ tsp. (1 package) active dry yeast
1¼ cup warm water
1 tsp. salt
2 Tbsp. extra virgin olive oil
¼ cup sprouted sesame seed
3¼ cups unbleached white flour

Directions
1. Put ¼ cup of warm water in a large warm bowl.
2. Sprinkle the yeast over the surface of the warm water and let it stand for ten minutes.

3. Add salt and olive oil to yeast and water mixture and whisk together.

4. Let stand for five minutes.

5. Whisk sprouted sesame seeds into liquid mixture.

6. Whisk flour into mixture ½ cup at a time. When the dough gets too stiff to whisk, use a wooden spoon.

7. Mix flour in until dough comes away from the sides of the bowl.

8. Turn dough out onto a lightly floured surface.

9. Knead with your hands until the dough is smooth and elastic.

10. Coat the inside of a large bowl with olive oil.

11. Place the dough in the oiled bowl and then flip it over so that the top is coated with olive oil.

12. Cover the bowl.

13. Allow the dough to rise in a warm location until doubled in volume (this should take one and a half to two hours).

While the dough is rising, prepare the topping.

14. In a bowl, combine 2 Tbsp. dried thyme, 4 Tbsp. sesame seeds, and one very finely chopped small white onion.

15. Heat a dry skillet over a medium heat and add the dried thyme, sesame seed, and onion mixture to the skillet.

16. Stir the skillet contents continuously until the mixture is slightly toasted.

17. Add salt and pepper to taste to the skillet mixture.

18. Remove skillet from heat and transfer skillet ingredients to bowl to cool.

19. Place a baking sheet in the oven.

20. Preheat oven to 450 degrees (with the baking sheet in the oven).

21. After the dough has doubled in volume, punch it down.

22. Turn it out onto a lightly floured surface and knead for about a minute.

23. Divide the dough into ten equal portions and roll them into a ball.

24. Lightly flour each dough ball and roll it into a circle about ¼ inch thick.

25. Place the rolled out dough circles on a lightly floured surface and cover with a towel.

26. Allow the dough to rise for 20 to 30 minutes.

27. After the dough has risen, brush the top of each circle with a light coat of olive oil.

28. Sprinkle the thyme and sesame mixture over the top of each coated dough circle.

29. Transfer the circles to the heated baking sheet in the oven with a spatula.

30. Bake for eight to ten minutes.

31. Remove from oven and allow the bread to cool slightly.

This bread is best eaten warm, shortly after it has been removed from the oven. If you serve this thyme bread as an appetizer at brunch or in the evening, try it with the sprouted eggplant (baba ghanouj) recipe in Chapter 6.

Sprouted Pumpkin Cinnamon Rolls

These take a little work, but the result is one that you will crave forever. This recipe yields 12 to 18 rolls.

Ingredients

For the dough:

¼ cup room temperature buttermilk

2½ tsp. (1 package) active dry yeast

1 cup (or one can) pumpkin puree

⅓ cup sugar

6 cups white unbleached bread flour

2 tsp. salt

6 large gently beaten eggs

1 cup (2 sticks) softened unsalted butter

For the filling:

¼ cup softened unsalted butter

½ cup light brown sugar

¼ cup white granulated sugar

1 Tbsp. cinnamon

½ cup chopped sprouted pumpkin seed (Alternatively, you can use
 chopped sprouted sunflower seeds or chopped soaked almonds.)

For the glaze:

½ cup confectioner's sugar

2 Tbsp. unsalted butter

1 tsp. pure vanilla extract

2 to 3 tsp. hot water (at least 110 degrees)

Directions

1. Put the buttermilk in a warm bowl.
2. Sprinkle the yeast over the surface of the warm buttermilk and let
    it stand for ten minutes. Whisk together the buttermilk and yeast
    and let it stand for five minutes.
3. Whisk the pumpkin puree and sugar into the buttermilk and
    yeast.
4. Add 1 cup of the flour, ½ cup at a time, to the pumpkin/butter-
    milk mixture. (This is best done with a mixer.)

5. Cover the mixing bowl and allow the mixture to sit in a warm place until bubbles form. (This should take about 45 minutes to an hour.).

6. Slowly add the rest of the flour and salt to the pumpkin mixture (The dough will be quite stiff.)

7. Add the eggs one at a time to the mixture.

8. Use a mixer fitted with dough hooks at a medium speed for two minutes to mix the eggs into the flour and pumpkin batter.

9. Increase mixer speed to medium and knead the dough for five minutes. The dough will be very stiff.

10. Turn the mixer speed to low.

11. Add the butter, 2 Tbsp. at a time, to the dough.

12. Scrape the sides of the bowl as you mix.

13. Knead until the dough is smooth, which should take about five minutes.

14. Prepare another bowl by coating the inside of it with butter.

15. Place the dough in the buttered bowl and then flip it over so that the top is coated with butter.

16. Cover the bowl and allow the dough to rise in a warm location until it is doubled in volume. (This should take one and a half to two hours.)

17. After the dough has doubled in volume, punch it down.

18. Turn it out onto a lightly floured surface and knead for about a minute.

19. Put the dough back in the bowl.

20. Cover the bowl and refrigerate for four to eight hours (or overnight).

21. Remove dough from fridge.

22. Preheat the oven to 350 degrees.

23. Prepare a large baking sheet by coating it with butter or vegetable oil.

24. In a medium-sized bowl, combine ½ cup light brown sugar, ¼ cup white granulated sugar, 1 Tbsp. cinnamon, and ½ cup chopped sprouted pumpkin seed.

25. Set sugar and sprouted pumpkin seed mixture aside.

26. Turn dough out onto a lightly floured surface and divide the dough evenly into thirds.

27. Roll the dough into a 12- by 8-inch rectangle with a floured rolling pin.

28. Spread butter over the surface of the rolled out dough with a pastry brush.

29. Spread a third of the sugar and sprouted pumpkin seed mixture over the surface of the rolled-out dough.

30. Starting from the long side, roll up the dough like a jelly roll and pinch the seam together.

31. Slice the roll into 1½-inch segments.

32. Place the cut segments horizontally on the prepared pan 2 inches apart from each other.

33. Continue steps 27 through 32 until you have made all the rolls.

34. Cover the rolls and allow them to rise for 45 minutes.

35. Bake the rolls at 350 degrees for about 17 to 20 minutes (or until golden brown).

36. Remove from oven and allow them to cool before glazing.

37. To make the glaze, combine ½ cup confectioner's sugar, 2 Tbsp. unsalted butter, and 1 tsp. pure vanilla extract and mix until smooth.

38. Add hot water to thin glaze if necessary.

39. Drizzle glaze over cooled rolls.

Great Sesame Granola

This recipe yields eight servings.

Ingredients

3 cups steel-cut oats (not instant)

3 cups warm water

6 Tbsp. buttermilk or yogurt

1 cup dried, unsweetened coconut

1 cup mixed dried fruit (raisins, dates, cranberries, blueberries, etc.)

1 cup sprouted and dried sesame seeds

1 cup any combination of soaked and dried almonds, sunflower seeds, and pumpkin seeds

½ cup sprouted wheat

½ cup coconut oil

¼ cup maple sugar

¼ cup honey or maple syrup

1 tsp. salt

Directions

1. The day before, put the oats in a large bowl with buttermilk or yogurt and the warm water.
2. Cover bowl of oats with a dish towel and allow the oats to sit at room temperature for 12 to 24 hours. (The buttermilk or yogurt will not go bad.)
3. After oats have sat for 12 to 24 hours, preheat oven to150 degrees (or its lowest setting).
4. Add the coconut, dried fruit, soaked and dried nuts/seeds, and sprouted wheat to the bowl of soaked oatmeal. Mix together with a wooden spoon.
5. In separate bowl, mix coconut oil, maple sugar, honey/maple syrup, and salt.

6. Add the coconut oil mixture into the bowl of oats and mix together with a wooden spoon.

7. Spread the mixture onto cookie sheets lined with parchment paper.

8. Bake in a 150 degree oven until crisp.

9. Break into pieces with your hands and store in an air-tight container.

Scoop of Granola

Sprouted Power Bars

Leave the granola bars on the supermarket shelves. These bars are truly a nutritious power food and are made with a combination of great sprouted grains, honey, and peanut butter. They will satisfy a sweet tooth and qualify as a well-rounded breakfast. If you want to make these power bars even sweeter, try adding dark chocolate chips.

This recipe yields 16 servings.

Ingredients

½ cup sprouted quinoa

½ cup sprouted oat groats (whole oat, not rolled)

¼ cup sprouted amaranth

5 soaked Medjool dates

2 Tbsp. peanut butter (The best to use is peanut butter that consists of only peanuts and perhaps a little salt.)

2 Tbsp. honey

½ cup soaked almonds

⅓ cup dried cranberries

2 Tbsp. popped amaranth (Directions for doing this are explained below.)

Butter (as needed)

Directions

1. To prepare popped amaranth:
   a. Place a skillet on the stove over high heat.
   b. Add 1 Tbsp. of peanut oil.
   c. Let the oil become hot enough that a drop of water dances and disappears when you drop it on the surface.
   d. Add ½ cup of amaranth into the skillet.
   e. Cover the skillet.
   f. Keep the skillet moving over the heat or stir until all of the amaranth has popped (about two minutes; you will be able to hear it).
   g. Remove the popped seeds from the skillet.
2. Coarse grind almonds in a food processor and empty into a dish.
3. Put dates, peanut butter, and honey in food processor and blend well.
4. Add almonds and blend.
5. Add grains and cranberries and blend.
6. Grease an 8-by-8-inch pan with butter.
7. Sprinkle half the popped amaranth on bottom of pan.
8. Spread grain mixture into pan and spread out.
9. Top with rest of popped amaranth.
10. Refrigerate until firm and then cut into 16 squares.

Sprouted Granola

This recipe yields eight to ten servings.

Ingredients

½ cup each of:

Sprouted buckwheat

Sprouted millet

Sprouted amaranth

Sprouted quinoa

Sprouted pumpkin seeds

Sprouted sunflower seeds

Soaked sesame seeds

Soaked flax seeds

Soaked currants

Soaked yellow raisins

1 cup soaked almonds

1 cup freeze-dried coconut

2 Tbsp. peanut oil

1 cup diced fresh strawberries

1 cup blueberries or cranberries

½ tsp. kosher salt

1 tsp. vanilla

4 Tbsp. honey or maple syrup

(Note: Adjust quantities according to taste.)

Directions

1. Sprout grains for two days and soak seeds for a few hours. Soak the dried fruit for about 30 minutes.
2. Mix all ingredients together in a large bowl and stir them well with a large spoon.

3. Preheat oven to 200 degrees.

4. Place a ½-inch layer of the seeds, dried fruit, and grain mixture on mesh dehydrator sheet or parchment paper and place on top of baking sheets.

5. Bake for two to four hours until granola is dry and crisp.

6. Allow to cool in oven. (Granola will get crisper as it cools.)

7. Remove from oven and break up into pieces.

Serve with milk, fresh nut milk, or soy milk.

There is a lot to be said for sending the kids (or yourself, for that matter) out the door in the morning knowing that they have had a wholesome breakfast. These recipes go beyond wholesome and offer you cereals, breads, baked goods, and breakfast bars that are not just good, but good for you. These recipes, like so many others offered in this book, are easily adaptable to many varied ingredients that you may wish to add or substitute. Now, to make that first meal even more perfect, try adding one of the juice items in the following chapter

Chapter 13

Beverages

You do not have to go to those fancy juice bars to get your wheatgrass juice anymore. Here are a variety of juice and smoothie recipes that are great meals and snacks.

Wheatgrass Juice

Another recipe that no book of this type would be complete without is wheatgrass juice. Wheatgrass juice has many health benefits. To start with, wheatgrass juice has extremely high levels of many vitamins and minerals, especially vitamin C, magnesium, calcium, and potassium. Wheatgrass also is chock full of chlorophyll, which helps oxygenate the blood and is believed to provide anti-inflammatory and antioxidant benefits.

Of course, wheatgrass is not a perfect food. The taste of wheatgrass has often been described as similar to mowed grass. Wheatgrass, in its straight form, can be an acquired taste. However, wheatgrass does blend well with other juices and its flavor is complementary to many other fruits and vegetables.

Note that any of the recipes included in this chapter can also be made with barley, oat, rye, or spelt grass. The drawback to barley grass is that it tastes even more like grass than wheatgrass does because wheatgrass has a sweet taste to it that barley grass does not. People that grow and drink barley grass often mix it with wheatgrass and the suggested mixture is five parts barley grass to one part wheatgrass. Oat seed is slightly more expensive than wheat and a little harder to grow. Rye is good as it tastes like wheat and is a very pretty grass. Any of these grasses can be made into juice.

If you are new to making your own juice, you may not have a juicer. A decent juicer can cost between $100 and $300. If you would like to experience wheatgrass before you invest in a juicer, you can juice wheatgrass using a blender. It is more labor intensive than using a juicer, but it will give you a decent product and allow you to enjoy some of these recipes without paying $200 just to try your own wheatgrass juice.

To make wheatgrass juice without a juicer, you will need a whole flat of wheatgrass grown according to the directions in Chapter 5. A standard flat will measure out to about 10 inches by 14 inches. The reason you will need an entire flat is because to use a blender, you will need to make a large quantity of juice. The juice a flat will yield will freeze, however.

Note that in most recipes for wheatgrass juice, the wheatgrass is measured by the size of a round increment. That is, a measurement of wheatgrass suggested for a recipe might be, "a 1-inch round of wheatgrass." The round is the diameter of a small bundle of wheatgrass.

Wheatgrass juice without a juicer

The trick to this recipe is to start by using a little water to get the juicing process going. Your goal is to have a juice that is as pure as possible. "Pure" here means a juice with as little added water as possible. To that end, you will begin by adding water and then "diluting" the water as much as possible with each successive step.

Ingredients

1 tray (approximately 10 by 14 inches) of wheatgrass

1 cup of water

Directions

1. Place a 1-inch round of wheatgrass and 1 cup of water into a blender.
2. Blend the mixture with a series of ten-second, high-speed bursts until the mixture is as liquefied as possible.
3. Line a colander with a double layer of cheesecloth.
4. Place the colander over a bowl to catch the juice that will be poured through it.
5. Pour the juice from the blender into the cheesecloth-lined colander.
6. Gather the cheesecloth together into a ball and squeeze the solids left behind in the cheesecloth into the bowl.
7. Add another 1-inch round of wheatgrass to the blender.
8. Pour the strained juice from the bowl into the blender.
9. Blend the mixture with a series of ten-second, high-speed bursts until the mixture is as liquefied as possible.
10. Pour the juice from the blender into the cheesecloth-lined colander.
11. Gather the cheesecloth together into a ball and squeeze the solids left behind in the cheesecloth into the bowl.
12. Repeat this procedure, using a cup of the strained juice over the 1-inch rounds of wheatgrass in the blender each time. You can continue to also add the solids left behind in the cheesecloth to the blender with each step.

13. When you have finished juicing the entire flat of wheatgrass, you can immediately freeze any of the juice you will use by pouring 1 ounce of wheatgrass juice into ice-cube trays

Of course, if you have a juicer you will follow the manufacturer's directions for juicing. In most cases, juicing wheatgrass with a juicer will call for adding water.

Now that you have straight wheatgrass, here are some excellent suggestions for tasty juice combinations. The fruit and/or vegetables you use in these recipes should be fresh, but if you consider making smoothies that use wheatgrass, frozen fruit is the best way to go. If you decided to use frozen fruit, your best option is to freeze fresh fruit 12 hours prior to making the smoothie. Frozen fruit is suggested for smoothies as a way of producing a good cold drink without having to add ice cubes.

Also, the recipes below can be made using either a juicer or a blender. If you choose to use a juicer, you can merely cut up the vegetables and feed them through your juicer. If you choose to use a blender, you should use some kind of liquid such as water or a small bit of juice. Also, if you use a blender it is advised that you should start with pre-juiced wheatgrass.

Veggie Green Wheat Juice

This recipe yields two juice servings.

Ingredients

3 stalks chopped celery

2 chopped medium cucumbers

A handful of spinach leaves (¼ to ½ cup)

½ cup fresh cilantro

3-inch round wheatgrass

Water as needed

Directions

Put everything through a juicer or into a blender and run it at high-
speed until liquefied.

Veggie Delight

This yields two servings.

Ingredients

3 stalks celery

2 large carrots

½ beet

A handful of spinach leaves (¼ to ½ cup)

½ cup alfalfa sprouts

½ cup fresh cilantro

3-inch round wheatgrass

Water as needed

Directions

Put everything through a juicer or into a blender and run it high-
speed until liquefied.

Cranapple–Grass

This yields two servings.

Ingredients

3 medium apples (Sweet apples are better than tart apples for this
recipe because this recipe includes cranberries, which are quite
tart.)

¼ cup cranberries

3-inch round wheatgrass

Honey to taste (if using a blender)

Cranberry juice or water as needed.

Directions

1.   Put everything through a juicer or into a blender and run it high speed until liquefied.

Note: If you make this recipe with a juicer, whisk the honey and cranberry juice in after you juice the apples, cranberries, and wheatgrass.

Fruitable–Grass

This recipe yileds two servings.

Ingredients

2 peeled and sectioned oranges

2 or 3 strawberries

2 large carrots

3-inch round wheatgrass

Directions

1.   Put everything through a juicer or into a blender and run it high speed until liquefied.

Wheatgrass Berry Blast

This recipe yields two servings.

Ingredients

1 orange

1 cup fresh berries

2-inch round wheatgrass

1 frozen banana

6 ounces non-fat yogurt

Honey (to taste)

Directions
1. Juice orange and wheatgrass.
2. Place juice and all other ingredients in a blender.
3. Blend until smooth.

Note: If you do not have a juicer, make the wheatgrass juice using a blender as explained earlier in the chapter, and add the rest of the ingredients to the blender with the wheatgrass after you juice the wheatgrass.

Wheat Grass Juice with Orange

Hearty Sprouty Smoothie

This recipe yields two servings.

Ingredients

1 cup wheat sprouts

1 cup millet sprouts

1 cup water

6 oz. non-fat yogurt

1 cup (more or less) orange or pineapple juice

2 frozen bananas chopped into 1-inch slices

Honey (to taste)

Directions

1. Soak wheat sprouts in water for three hours in the refrigerator.
2. Put all ingredients except honey in a blender.
3. Blend on high until it is thick like a shake.
4. If the shake is too thick, add more juice.
5. Add honey to taste as blender runs.

Pineapple and Sprout Smoothie

This yields two servings.

Ingredients

12 oz. frozen pineapple

1 peeled and sectioned orange

1 to 2 cups orange or pineapple juice

4 oz. plain non-fat yogurt

2 Tbsp. honey

½ cup alfalfa sprouts

1 cup sunflower sprouts

½ cup clover sprouts

Directions

1. Blend pineapple, orange, pineapple juice, and yogurt for about one minute.
2. Add honey and blend about 30 seconds.
3. Add sprouts and blend to desired consistency.
4. You can add more juice if it is too thick.

Rejuvelac

Rejuvelac is a fermented drink that is made from grains and is used, primarily, as a digestive aid. Rejuvelac had beneficial bacteria as a result of its fermentation process and is considered to be probiotic. Foods that are probiotic contain beneficial bacteria, similar to the kind that is found naturally in your body. Probiotic foods aid in digestion and protect against harmful bacteria. If you have never had rejuvelac, you should begin by drinking 4 ounces a day for a couple days and then drink 8 ounces a day. This helps accustom your system to the increase in beneficial bacteria.

This recipe yields two servings.

Ingredients

1½ cups sprouted whole millet
1 Tbsp. raisins or dried cranberries
Spring water

Directions

1. Rinse and drain millet well.
2. Lightly pound the millet with a pestle in a mortar to bruise the grains.
3. Place the sprouted millet in a large glass jar.
4. Fill the jar no more than ⅔ full with fresh spring water.
5. Add 1 Tbsp. raisins or dried cranberries.
6. Tightly close the jar.
7. Ferment for two to three days. Gently shake the jar once each day.

Oat Sprout Almond Milk

This milk is a meal in itself as it is filled with nutrition. It is great at breakfast with or on a bowl of fruit.

This recipe yields four servings.

Ingredients

2 cups sprouted oats

½ to ¾ cup soaked almonds

4 cups water (spring water is the best)

1 Tbsp. honey

Vanilla (to taste)

Directions

1. Blanch almonds by placing them in a bowl and pouring hot water over them.
2. Remove almonds from hot water after a minute or two and remove outer skin. Set the almonds aside.
3. Place oat sprouts in blender with half the water.
4. Blend on a medium speed for one minute.
5. Add remainder of water and blend another minute.
6. Pour blended liquid though cheesecloth or a strainer.
7. Rinse blender and return strained liquid to the blender.
8. Add remaining ingredients to blender and blend on medium speed for one minute.
9. Blend on low speed for five minutes.
10. Chill the milk before enjoying.

Almond Chai

This recipe yields two servings.

Ingredients

3 cups oat sprout almond milk (see previous recipe) or coconut milk

½ Tbsp. ginger juice (The easiest way to make juice is simply by processing the ginger root in the small bowl of a food processor, then squeezing the pulp in a small piece of cheesecloth. Use about a 1-inch piece of ginger root.)

¼ tsp. nutmeg ground

½ Tbsp. cinnamon

1½ Tbsp. carob powder

½ tsp. ground cardamom

2 Tbsp. pure maple syrup

Pinch of fresh ground black pepper

Directions

1. Place all ingredients in a blender and blend on high until smooth.
2. Serve immediately.

Almond Nog

This recipe yields six servings.

Ingredients

2 cups soaked almonds

½ cup pine nuts (unsoaked)

5 cups unchlorinated spring water

3 frozen bananas

6 pitted dates

½ tsp. nutmeg

½ tsp. ground cloves

1 tsp. vanilla extract

2 tsp. almond oil

Directions

1. Place the soaked almonds, pine nuts, and 5 cups of spring water in a blender and blend on high speed until smooth.
2. Line a colander with a fine cheesecloth and place the colander over a bowl.
3. Pour the contents of the blender into the cheesecloth-lined colander.
4. Bring the corners of the cheesecloth together to form a bag.
5. Squeeze the bag, allowing the liquid to flow into the bowl, until all the liquid is squeezed out.
6. Set the liquid aside.
7. Place the frozen bananas, dates, nutmeg, ground cloves, vanilla extract, and almond oil in the blender.
8. Pour the liquid contents of bowl over the contents of the blender and blend the mixture together on high.

Serve this drink immediately.

Now that you have enjoyed a full complement of breakfast, lunch, and dinner with healthy sprouts, it is about time for dessert.

Chapter 14

Desserts

I t is only fitting that you cap a wonderful meal made with healthy sprouts with a sweet treat that is also made with sprouts. Here are some classics as well as some new recipes that are sure to please.

Carrot Almond Cake

If you use the ground almonds in this recipe, this is a flourless cake that is dense and delicious, especially with the cream cheese frosting.

This recipe yields eight servings.

Ingredients

1½ cups steamed and pureed carrots

6 eggs, separated

2 cups honey or brown sugar

½ cup chopped soaked almonds

½ cup raisins

2 Tbsp. ground almonds or flour

1 tsp. grated orange zest

1 tsp. salt

1 Tbsp. ground cardamom

Cream cheese frosting (optional)

Directions

1. Preheat your oven to 350 degrees.
2. Butter a 9-inch cake pan (round or square).
3. Combine pureed carrots, egg yolks, and honey or sugar in a large bowl.
4. Mix ground almonds or flour, soaked almonds, raisins, orange zest, salt, and cardamom into carrot mixture.
5. Beat egg whites in a separate bowl until stiff.
6. Gently fold stiff egg whites into carrot mixture.
7. Spread batter into buttered cake pan.
8. Bake at 350 degrees for about 45 minutes or until springy.
9. Cool to room temperature and then refrigerate.
10. Frost with cream cheese frosting if desired.

For cream cheese frosting:

Ingredients

8 oz. cold cream cheese

5 Tbsp. softened unsalted butter

2 tsp. vanilla

2 cups sifted powdered sugar (Sift after measuring.)

Directions

1. With a mixer, beat 8 oz. cold cream cheese with 5 Tbsp. softened unsalted butter and 2 tsp. vanilla until combined.
2. Gradually add 2 cups powdered sugar about ¼ cup at a time.
3. Continue to add sifted powdered sugar until you reach a consistency and sweetness that suits your taste.

Carrot Sunflower Sprout Cake ——————.

Here is a more traditional carrot spice cake with sunflower seed sprouts. This recipe yields eight servings.

Ingredients

1 cup grated carrots (about 2 large carrots)

1 cup raisins

1½ cups sugar

1 tsp. cinnamon

1 tsp. nutmeg

½ tsp. ground cloves

1½ cups water

3 Tbsp. butter

1 cup sprouted sunflower seeds

2 cups unbleached all-purpose flour

2 tsp. baking soda

¼ tsp. salt

Directions

1. Put grated carrots, raisins, sugar, cinnamon, nutmeg, ground cloves, water, and butter in a medium sauce pan.

2. Heat carrot mixture over medium-high heat until boiling. Boil mixture for five minutes, remove from heat, and allow to cool slightly.

3. Place mixture into a large mixing bowl.

4. Allow carrot mixture to cool completely (which will take several hours, or slightly less if you place it in the refrigerator).

5. Preheat oven to 325 degrees.

6. Prepare a 9-by-13-inch cake pan by coating the inside of it with butter or vegetable shortening and a fine coat of flour.

7. Sift 2 cups of flour, baking soda, and salt together in a bowl.

8. Add flour mixture and sunflower seed sprouts to carrot mixture.

9. Stir batter only enough to incorporate flour and sunflower seed sprouts into carrot mixture. Do not over-beat.

10. Pour batter into prepared cake pan.

11. Bake at 325 degrees for about one hour (until top springs back when lightly touched).

12. Cool and serve from pan.

This can be iced with cream cheese icing (see previous recipe).

Almond and Coconut Creme Fruit Parfait

This yields six servings.

Ingredients

½ cup soaked cashews

2 cups coconut meat

½ to ¼ cup coconut milk

¼ cup pitted dates pitted

1½ tsp. vanilla bean (about 1 bean)

2 Tbsp. carob powder (Carob is a bean that is similar in nature to chocolate.)

2 cups fresh diced pineapple, orange, and banana

2 Tbsp. orange juice

1 tsp. cinnamon

Directions

1. Place soaked cashews, coconut meat, coconut milk, date, vanilla bean, and carob powder in a blender and blend on high speed until smooth.

2. Toss diced fruit with orange juice and cinnamon.

3. Layer blended cashew/coconut mixture and diced fruit in six parfait cups.
4. Chill in the refrigerator.

Garnish with sprig of mint just prior to serving.

Sprouted Granola and Zucchini Torte

Use the sprouted granola found earlier in Chapter 12 for this wonderful dessert. This yields eight servings.

Ingredients

1 cup finely chopped unpeeled zucchini

1 Tbsp. fresh lemon juice

1 cup lightly crushed sprouted granola

½ cup chopped soaked almonds

¾ cup unbleached flour

1½ tsp. baking powder

¼ tsp. salt

1 tsp. cinnamon

2 eggs

¾ cup sugar

1 tsp. vanilla

Directions

1. Preheat oven to 325 degrees.
2. Prepare a 9-by-9-inch cake pan by coating the inside of it with butter or vegetable shortening and a fine coat of flour.
3. In a mixing bowl, combine zucchini and fresh lemon juice.
4. In a separate bowl, sift together flour, baking powder, salt, and cinnamon.

5. In a separate bowl, beat eggs well.

6. Add sugar to egg mixture and beat well until eggs and sugar are fluffy.

7. Add flour mixture from step 4 to egg and sugar mixture.

8. Mix flour, egg, and sugar until you have a smooth batter.

9. Add zucchini, granola, sprouted almonds, and vanilla to batter and blend well.

10. Spread batter in prepared cake pan.

11. Bake torte at 325 degrees for 40 minutes or until the top develops a puffed crust.

12. Cool in pan.

13. Cut into squares in pan.

Serve torte topped with fruit and/or whipped cream.

Pumpkin Pudding with Pumpkin Seed Sprouts and Walnuts

This recipe yields four servings.

Ingredients

½ cup sugar

½ cup water

1 lb. of cubed sugar pumpkin

⅓ cup finely chopped sprouted pumpkin seeds

⅓ cup finely chopped walnuts

1 Tbsp. lemon juice

1 cup heavy cream or non-fat yogurt

Directions

1. In a sauce pan over a low heat, dissolve sugar in water.

2. Increase heat and bring to a boil, stirring constantly for five to ten minutes. The mixture will thicken. Do not allow it to caramelize (brown).
3. After sugar thickens, stir in pumpkin cubes.
4. Cover the pan and reduce the heat to low. Cook for one minute then uncover.
5. Continue to simmer over low heat, stirring occasionally, until pumpkin is cooked and absorbed almost all of the syrup.
6. Stir in chopped sprouted pumpkin seeds and chopped walnuts.
7. Spoon into four individual serving bowls.

Serve warm or chill. You can top with heavy cream or non-fat yogurt.

Wheat Sprout Chocolate Cream Pie

After you sample this recipe, you will never feel guilty about having dessert again. This chocolate cream pie recipe is healthy whether you have it with your morning coffee, as a mid-afternoon snack, after dinner, or as a midnight snack.

You can also serve the filling of this pie as a pudding. Simply omit the pit crust and pour the filling into individual serving bowls, chill for two hours, and serve topped with chopped sprouted almonds and powdered sugar. This recipe will give you eight delicious servings.

Ingredients

2 cups sprouted wheat

3 Tbsp. unsweetened natural cocoa powder

4 Tbsp. vanilla flavored custard powder (If you do not have custard powder, you can substitute corn starch and ½ tsp. of vanilla.)

½ cup sugar

1½ cups whole milk

1 cup chopped soaked almonds

Powdered sugar

Directions for filling

1. Place sprouted wheat, cocoa powder, and custard powder in the bowl of a food processor and process to a smooth paste, adding water if necessary.

2. Pour milk into a heavy bottom saucepan.

3. Add sugar to the saucepan with the milk.

4. Heat the milk along with the sugar over a medium-high heat to 180 degrees, stirring continuously.

5. Add the sprouted wheat, cocoa powder, and custard paste to the milk and sugar.

6. Stir the mixture continuously until it thickens. (This should take about ten minutes.)

7. Remove saucepan from heat and set aside to cool.

8. Prepare pie crust.

Soaked almond pie crust

Ingredients

2 cups soaked almonds

½ cup pitted soft (or soaked) dates

¼ cup raisins

Juice from ½ orange

1 Tbsp. orange zest

Cinnamon to taste

Directions

1. Place all ingredients in the bowl of a food processor and process until they form a loose meal.

2.   Transfer ingredients to a 9-inch pie plate and press into pie plate.

3.   Pour the filling from the bowl you set aside into the crust.

4.   Cover pie and allow it to chill for one to two hours.

5.   Top with chopped soaked almonds and powdered sugar.

Try filling the almond crust with this very different pumpkin pie filling.

Raw Pumpkin Pie Filling ———————————•

This recipe yields eight servings.

Ingredients

2 cups raw pumpkin

1 cup soaked almonds

2 to 4 Tbsp. fresh lemon or orange juice

2 Tbsp. honey

½ cup shaved coconut

½ cup soaked raisins (Soak raisins in water for about an hour.)

½ tsp. dried ginger powder

1 Tbsp. grated fresh ginger

1 tsp. cinnamon

¼ tsp. nutmeg

Directions

1.   Combine the pumpkin, soaked almonds, juice, and honey in a blender and blend on high until smooth.

2.   Add coconut, raisins, ginger powder, grated ginger, cinnamon, and nutmeg and blend another ten seconds. The mixture should be the consistency of thick pancake batter.

3.   If mixture is too thin, add more almonds.

4.   Pour batter into soaked almond pie crust.

5.   Cover and chill eight to 12 hours.

Serve topped with chopped almonds and powdered sugar.

You are now free to enjoy sprouts at every meal and snack throughout your day. Breakfast, brunch, lunch, dinner, or a midnight snack can offer you the healthy benefits of sprouts. Do not forget that you do not have to enjoy sprouts in recipes, but just as they are, plain and simple. Sprouts are simply delicious. And while you are sharing, do not forget to share with your pets.

Chapter 15

Sprouts for Your Pets

Whether your furry best friend is a dog or a cat, or your pet friend has feathers or scales, you will find that adding sprouts and/or shoots to its diet will improve its health in the same ways that it has yours. Sprouts provide vitamins, carbohydrates, protein, and fat for your pets in the same way that they do for you.

When choosing seeds to sprout for your pets, use the same guidelines that you use when choosing seeds to sprout for yourself. You should choose organic seeds that have not been treated with chemicals. Follow the same growing guidelines that you follow when you grow sprouts for yourself and your family. Make sure that your equipment is clean and that you are safe in your procedures.

Grass

You read about growing wheatgrass and other types of fresh greens in soil in Chapter 5. The grass you grow for your pets is exactly the same as the wheat, oat, or rye grass that you will grow for yourself.

If you have a cat, you know how much your feline friend enjoys eating grass to aid in digestion. Growing grass for your cat will ensure that it gets a good, clean, and healthy vegetable. Your dog may enjoy eating grass, as well.

If you are a cat owner, you are probably familiar with the term "cat grass." This is not a particular type of grass but grass that you grow for your cat to eat. Cat grass could be any type of cereal grass that has been described in this book (wheatgrass, oat grass, rye grass, or barley grass). Your cat (or dog) will choose for itself the type of grass that it prefers to eat. Pets can be just as picky or accepting as people can. It is all a matter of taste and preference.

Cats are natural carnivores that may supplement their diet with greens such as grass. Not all cats will eat grass, but grass does aid in a cat's digestion. Cats that do not eat grass are probably getting something else in their diets that aid their digestion.

You will know that your cat may enjoy eating grass if you notice that it is nibbling on your houseplants or if you notice that it is eating the grass of your yard. Grass that you grow for your cat is healthier than either of these options. The grass on your lawn may have pesticides, herbicides, or unhealthy fertilizers on it, and your houseplants may be toxic to cats in some way.

By establishing cat grass in your home, you are offering a very healthy alternative to your houseplants and your lawn. When you establish cat grass, you will probably notice that your cat will prefer the cat grass to your houseplants and will stop munching on the grass in your yard. Your cat will appreciate the clean, sweet taste of your efforts.

When you grow grass for your cats, grow in the same manner that you would for yourself. Be sure that you grow it in a low container that your cat will not be able to tip over easily. You may think about growing the grass in smaller trays than you might grow it in for your own use. The smaller trays make it easier to set out for your cat or remove it if you notice that your pet is eating too much.

Another reason for a low container that is hard to tip over is that a cat has a carnivore's teeth. A cat's teeth are not made for grazing, but for tearing up meat. This means that when a cat eats grass, it needs to tear it off as opposed to chewing it off. A low, bottom-heavy container will decrease the chance of the grass and dirt being spilled as the cat rips the grass out to eat it.

If you begin to notice that your cat is regurgitating a lot of the grass, remove it from their access regularly because this is a sign your cat is eating too much of the grass. Put it out for limited times on a regular basis.

While the types of grass included in this book are commonly referred to as cat grass, it is a well-known fact that dogs eat grass, as well. Dogs are more omnivorous than cats and are more likely to eat vegetation than cats are. So growing grass for your dog makes as much sense as growing it for a cat. If you grow for your dog, do so in low containers that are hard to tip over.

Whether you are growing grass for a dog or a cat, you should keep in mind that with each regrowth (that is, the growth that occurs after the grass has been chewed down), the grass will get a little tougher. With this in mind, you should only allow the grass two or three regrowths before you offer fresh new grass to your pet. The new grass is more tender and easier to digest.

The focus here has been on grass for cats and dogs, but you may have other pets that eat greens. Rabbits, gerbils, hamsters, and many other pets appreciate fresh green grass in their diet.

Sprouts

Some pets, like humans, will show sensitivity to wheat. If this is the case with your pet, you can offer it sprouts. Even if your pet shows that it can tolerate wheat, sprouts offer your pet a wonderful and healthy alternative food source.

Barley sprouts, rye sprouts, and sunflower sprouts are a good place to start when it comes to offering your pet fresh sprouts. Like any of the cereal grasses, you will grow the sprouts for your pet in the same way that you grow them for yourself and your family.

The preferred growing method for sprouts that will be offered to a dog or cat is the tray method. The reason for this is that once the sprouts are ready, you already have them in a low container that you can move to the floor for your pet's grazing needs. For you and your pet, it is a matter of convenience.

There are other sprouts that are as beneficial to your pets as they are to you. Alfalfa sprouts, broccoli sprouts, lentil sprouts, and mung bean sprouts can be added to your pet's diet. When adding these sprouts to your pet's diet, you should grind them up and mix them into your pet's food just prior to serving so the sprouts will still offer the same living nutrition. Talk to your veterinarian about how much you should mix into your pet's diet. Whether or not your pet accepts the sprouts in its food will depend on your pet's taste.

If you have birds, you are probably already feeding them seeds. You can also offer your birds a sprout alternative for their diet. Sprouted fennel, millet, mustard, quinoa, radish, and sesame are great choices for small birds such as finches, canaries, and cockatiels. Again, choose and sprout these seeds the same way you would for yourself and your family.

Conclusion

It is quite amazing that sprouts, shoots, and greens can be grown so simply with just a little bit of time and space. As you review the directions and recipes noted throughout this book, you will be amazed at the great variety of fresh foods that you can produce in your very own home.

The common advice most case study participants give is that the best way to learn how to grow sprouts is to just do it and keep trying until you get it right. There is no substitute for experience. The amazing thing you may have already discovered is just how simple growing sprouts really is.

It is also amazing at just how flavorful and fresh sprouts are. Whether you enjoy the mild nuttiness of alfalfa sprouts, or the slightly hot bite of radish sprouts, you will begin to think about how you might use sprouts in more and more of your daily meal planning. Do not be afraid to experiment with the recipes included in this book. The recipes are meant to be a launching point for your own culinary creativity. Substitute sprouts, vegetables, stocks, or anything else in any of the recipes to suit your own tastes.

If you have the opportunity to purchase sprouts in your local grocery store, do so to compare them to your own homegrown sprouts. If you have a local farmer's market in your town, visit with the farmers that sell sprouts and talk to them about their best practices. You will be pleasantly surprised by their willingness to talk about all things sprouts. You will learn a good deal by talking to people that grow sprouts on a daily basis. The people who grow sprouts are passionate about doing so and most are quite eager to talk about it.

Besides the advice of experimenting with a variety of sprout types, also heed the many warnings about cleanliness because it is of vital importance. Go the extra mile to make sure that all of your working surfaces and utensils are sterile prior to starting. These preparations will save your sprouts as well as the health of those that enjoy your lovingly grown greens. As you ensure the cleanliness of your kitchen, also make sure that you work with the freshest products available. Read labels and expiration dates. Learn as much as you can about where your ingredients come from.

Get to know those businesses listed in the Appendix of this book. In the beginning, try to buy your seeds from a variety of sources to see who you like working with and which seeds work the best for you. If you live in an area where you have access to organic seeds direct from the farmer, give it a try. There is a lot to be said for community supported agriculture.

Finally, share your "crops" with your family, friends, and neighbors. The gift of food, especially fresh food, is a wonderful gift.

Appendix A

Resources

Seeds and Equipment

Backyard Style

This online dealer of lawn and yard products has a good selection of indoor greenhouses and greenhouse equipment and material.

www.backyardstyle.com

1-866-331-1920

Canning Pantry

This company offers Mason Jars and a good variety of home sprouting equipment.

www.canningpantry.com

1-800-285-9044

Mini Greenhouse Kits

This company is a great source for a wide variety of small indoor green-houses.

www.minigreenhousekits.com

1-866-606-3911

Mumm's Sprouting Seeds

Mumm's Sprouting Seeds is a certified organic sprouting seed supplier.

www.sprouting.com

306-747-2935

Sproutman

Sproutman, also known as Steve Meyerowitz, is one of the world's leading experts and proponents of sprout growing and consumption. At his Web site, you can find a huge selection of sprout growing materials such as hemp sprout bags, automatic sprouters, and juicers.

http://sproutman.com/

SproutPeople

SproutPeople is a great source of seeds, sprouts, equipment, and information about sprouting.

www.sproutpeople.com

1- 877-777-6887

TN Farm Supply

This company is a good source for inexpensive indoor greenhouses.

http://tnfarmsupply.com/

WheatgrassKits.com

This site offers a complete selection of kits, wheatgrass juicers, certified organic seeds, and supplies to grow wheat grass, barley grass, herbs, sprouts, greens, and edible mushrooms. They also carry soymilk kits, composting supplies, books and more.

www.wheatgrasskits.com

1-866-948-4727

Glossary

Antioxidant: Any substance that inhibits and reverses the destructive effects of oxidation in the body. Oxidation creates free radicals that have a damaging effect on cells.

Biogenic: Something necessary for maintaining the basic life processes.

Calorie: The measurement or unit of the energy producing potential in food.

Carbohydrate: An organic compound derived from carbon, hydrogen, and oxygen that is an essential source of nutrition for humans and animals. The three common types of carbohydrates in food are sugars, starches, and dietary fiber.

Chlorophyll: The green and purple pigment in plants that is responsible for capturing the energy necessary for photosynthesis.

Cotyledon: The inner part of a seed that contains stored energy used for growth.

Enzyme: Proteins produced in living cells that speed up or increase the rate of a chemical reaction such as the metabolic processes of an organism.

Germinate: To start to grow from a seed.

Humus: Partially decomposed organic matter that is the source of nutrients for plant life.

Mineral: Inorganic matter that must be consumed by plants or animals to remain healthy.

Mucilaginous: A type of seed that produces a moist and sticky glue that acts as a protective coating.

Phenolic compound: Chemical compounds that are essential to the growth of plants and have been shown to have a wide array of health benefits to humans.

Photosynthesis: The process green plants use to produce simple carbohydrates, using energy that chlorophyll captures.

Phytoestrogen: Compounds that plants produce and have similar characteristics to the human hormone estrogen. These phytoestrogens, namely isoflavones, coumestans, and lignans, have been shown to help guard against osteoporosis, cancer, and heart disease.

Plumule: The undeveloped primary shoot of a plant embryo.

Protein: A complex molecule found in plant and animal cells. Proteins have high molecular weight and contain carbon, hydrogen, oxygen, nitrogen, and sulfur. Protein is vital to the structure and function of all cells.

Radicle: A young plant root.

Shoot: A newly grown part of a plant that has emerged from a seed.

Sprout: To begin to grow from a seed, grain, legume, or nut. The new growth from a seed, grain, legume, or nut.

Sulforaphane: A natural cancer-fighting compound that helps support antioxidants such as vitamins C and E. Broccoli sprouts contain very high amounts of sulforaphane.

Testa: The coat or shell of a seed.

Toxin: A naturally occurring poison produced by a living organism, such as bacteria.

Vitamin: Any of a variety of organic substances necessary to the nutrition and normal metabolism of most animals and humans.

Bibliography

Braunstein, Mark, Sprout Garden, Indoor Grower's Guide to Gourmet Sprouts, Summertown, TN, Book Publishing Company, 1999.

Cupillard, Valerie, Sprouts and Sprouting, The Complete Guide with Seventy Healthy and Creative Recipes, London, England, Grub Street, 2007.

Meyerowitz, Steve, Sprouts, The Miracle Food, Great Barrington, MA, Sproutman Publications, 2008.

O'Bannon, Kathleen, Sprouts, The Savory Source for Health and Vitality, Summertown, TN, Alive Books, 2000.

USDA National Nutrient Database for Standard Reference, **www.nal. usda.gov/fnic/foodcomp/search**, accessed April 18, 2010.

Wigmore, Ann, The Sprouting Book: How to Grow and Use Sprouts to Maximize Your Health and Vitality, Avery Books, 1986.

Author's Biography

Richard Helweg has more than 25 years experience working in the non-profit sector as an artistic director, managing director, and executive director. He is an award-winning playwright and has recently written *...And Justice for All, A History of the Supreme Court*, a book for young readers and *How to Get Your Share of the $30-Plus Billion Being Offered by U.S. Foundations*. Richard lives in Lincoln, Nebraska with his wife, Karen, and sons Aedan and Rory.

Richard Helweg

Index

D

Detoxification, 21

E

Enzymes, 19-20, 26, 28, 57-58, 118, 161, 14

F

Fat, 222, 271, 150, 162

Fenugreek, 46, 52, 57-58, 75, 121, 124, 7

Flax, 21-22, 247, 35-36, 57-58, 72, 79

G

Garbanzo, 43, 46, 52, 75, 173

Garlic, 22, 176-178, 181-183, 187-190, 192-193, 198-199, 201-202, 204, 206, 208-209, 212, 214-215, 218-219, 224-225, 78, 80, 87, 102, 107, 110-113, 120-121, 124, 129, 132, 135-146, 148-149, 152-153, 158-160, 163, 169-170, 173-174, 6

Germination, 19, 25-26, 33, 70, 72-73, 161-162

Glucoraphanin, 161-162

Grass, 278, 249-250, 253-255, 271-273, 74, 89-91, 9-10

Greenhouse, 277, 40-41, 95-96, 15, 5

Green pea, 46, 52, 75, 144, 7

H

Hull, 53

Humus, 94, 280

J

The Jar Method, 35, 60, 64, 67, 78-80

L

Lathyrogen, 49

Lettuce, 39, 46, 52-53, 75, 80, 84-85, 131-132, 161-162, 13-14

Lentil, 21, 198-200, 274, 46, 52, 75, 100, 119-120, 159, 161-162, 166, 169-170, 7-8

Living seed, 18

M

Mineral, 23, 39, 280

Mucilaginous, 72, 79, 280

Mung, 21-22, 175, 177-180, 182-183, 194, 196, 201, 214-217, 223-224, 274, 42-43, 47, 52, 57-58, 76, 79, 100, 118, 125, 153-155, 157-158, 161-162, 170, 14, 7-8

Mustard, 183, 186-187, 224-226, 274, 47, 52, 59, 68, 76, 84-85, 106, 108-109, 127, 131, 161-162, 9

N

National Organic Program, 42

O

Oats, 227-229, 233-235, 237, 244-245, 258, 47, 52, 76, 89

Onion, 22, 176, 178, 180-183, 185, 187-188, 194, 198-199, 201-202, 212-215, 218-222, 239, 47, 52, 76, 87, 100, 102, 107, 116-117, 124,